AQA

FUNCTIONAL SKILLS
ENGLISH

Pass Level 2

David Stone

Highly experienced Senior Examiner

www.pearsonschoolsandfecolleges.co.uk

✓ Free online support
✓ Useful weblinks
✓ 24 hour online ordering

0845 630 33 33

D0774015

Heinemann

Part of Pearson

Contents

Section B Writing   Introduction to Writing

Introduction

What is the purpose of this book?

The purpose of this book is to prepare you so that you pass the Level 2 examination in Functional Skills English: Reading, Writing, and Speaking, Listening and Communication. There is also a section on Level 1 Reading, Writing, Speaking, Listening and Communication. You can achieve a certificate at Level 1 if this is more suited to your abilities.

Achieving Functional Skills English at Level 2 will show that you are able to apply the skills you need in English to help gain the most from life, learning and work. The kind of reading and writing you will be doing is functional. It's about everyday reading and writing in the world. There is no literature – poems, plays, novels or drama – in Functional Skills English; it is about leaflets, brochures, articles, letters, reports, graphs and tables (see the examples opposite). Some of these you need to be able to understand and some of these you will have to write.

The Speaking, Listening and Communication part of Functional Skills English you will be doing with your teacher or tutor in class.

The idea for Functional Skills first came from the people in industry and the world of work who will be employing you, so getting the qualification will help you get a good job.

The purpose of this book is to:

▶ explain exactly what you have to do to achieve Level 1 and Level 2 in the Functional Skills English examination in Reading and Writing

▶ give you examples and practice activities in the skills you will be tested on

▶ provide sample tests in Reading and Writing with some suggestions for what you might do in class for Speaking, Listening and Communication.

If you can follow and achieve good results in the activities and tests in the book, you should pass the Level 2 Functional Skills in English examination.

Darfur is one of the driest parts of Su – so dry that sometimes rain falls just two hours, in the whole yea

That's just 40mm of rain to last all year (in the UK, we get an average of 1,200mm). Families in Sudan everything they can to grow en food to eat, but without wate crops wither and die – and pe do too, in their thousands.

But something's happenir Small banks of earth are appearing, curving across land. And inside each cur crops are growing, green healthy, enough to to fee family all year round.

These earth banks are call terraces, and each forms a – a simple shape that holds vital water, and pushes hunc You can help another family b with Practical Action.

Make a gift for the tools

20 high

DofE | The Duke of Edinburgh's Award

http://www.dofe.org/What_is_a_DofE_prog.aspx

What is a DofE programme?

A DofE programme is a real adventure from beginning to end. It doesn't matter who you are or where you're from. You just need to be aged between 14 and 24 and realise there's more to life than sitting on a sofa watching life pass you by.

You can do programmes at three levels, Bronze, Silver or Gold, which lead to a Duke of Edinburgh's Award.

You'll find yourself helping people or the community, getting fitter, developing skills, going on an expedition and taking part in a residential activity.

But here's the best bit – you get to choose what you do!

Why should I do it?

Good question!

Because, from the first day to the last it's a real adventure. Every section gives you something different – that's the fun of it!

You'll enjoy loads of new experiences, ...alents you never thought you had, ...yourself and meet lots of people ...ou. Also, you'll do things you love ...kick... of. It's a real buzz!

How do I get the Award?

You achieve an Award by completing a personal programme of activities in four sections (five if you're going for Gold). These sections are:

- Volunteering – helping someone, your community or the environment
- Physical – becoming fitter through sport, dance or fitness activities
- Skills – developing existing talents or trying something new
- Expedition – planning, training for and completing an adventurous journey
- Residential (Gold only) – staying and working away from ...e... part of a team.

...to spend on each section ...doing.

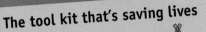

The tool kit that's saving lives

...his local spade, ...alled a Kodal, is ...sed to dig a ...rench...

...the soil is piled up into a crescent shape with a fork...

...and an A-frame checks that each terrace is level.

...venue generating football clubs in the world

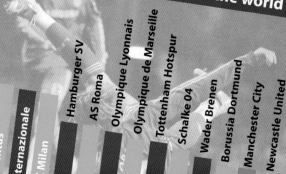

Liverpool | Juventus | Internazionale | AC Milan | Hamburger SV | AS Roma | Olympique Lyonnais | Olympique de Marseille | Tottenham Hotspur | Schalke 04 | Wader Brenen | Borussia Dortmund | Manchester City | Newcastle United

---

http://careersforyou.com

Careers for you

- ▶ Careers Advice Home
- ▶ Start Here
- ▶ In Your Region
- ▶ Find A Course
- ▶ Career Tools
- ▶ Jobs and Careers
- ▶ Help and Advice
- ▶ Podcasts
- ▶ Other Languages
- ▶ Get In Touch
- ▶ Discussion Forums

Restaurant or Catering Manager

I'm helping children get healthy by cooking good, nutritious school dinners.

What is the work like?

Restaurant and catering managers are responsible for making sure customers are satisfied with the quality of food and service provided in a range of eating places.

As a restaurant manager, you could work in catering outlets such as: hotels, small independent restaurants, eateries that are part of a large chain, and fast-food outlets. You would be front-of-house, welcoming customers to the restaurant and showing them to their table.

As a catering manager you would work in larger catering operations, such as business or factory canteens, hospitals or schools. You would have less contact with customers than a restaurant manager, and spend more time behind the scenes.

Your duties as a restaurant or catering manager would include:

- planning healthy, nutritious menus
- ensuring good, efficient service to customers
- running the business in line with strict hygiene, health and safety guidelines
- ensuring a high standard of service and presentation
- making sure all staff are fully trained
- keeping staff motivated
- organising shift patterns and rotas
- managing stock control and budgets
- advertising vacancies and recruiting staff.

What qualifications and experience will employers look for?

To apply for a trainee manager post, you will usually need a good general standard of education plus relevant experience.

Another way you could get into a management position would be to work your way up. For example, you could start as a waiter/waitress and with experience and qualifications (such as an NVQ Level 3 in Food Service Advanced Craft), you could take on more responsibilities, supervising less-experienced colleagues. You would then be in a good position to apply for a trainee management post.

...hains run management trainee schemes that can lead to restaurant or catering ...and some employers will accept you with A-levels or a BTEC National award. Fast-...catering companies and large restaurants may also run management trainee schemes.

What are the Functional English skill standards?

The skill standards are really a list of things you need to be able to master in order to achieve Level 1 or Level 2.

There are three parts to Functional Skills English, just like there are for GCSE English:

▶ Speaking, Listening and Communication – which you do in school or college, marked by your teacher or tutor

▶ Reading ⎤ which are assessed in an external
▶ Writing ⎦ examination marked by an examiner.

These are done separately. You have to pass each of these three parts in order to get the Functional Skills English certificate. Look at the tables on pages vi and vii. These set out all of the skill standards for Level 1 and then for Level 2.

Level 1

Look at the Level 1 part first. The first column gives you the skill standard you are trying to achieve. So, if you pass at Level 1, you will be able to:

▶ take full part in formal and informal discussions and exchanges that include unfamiliar subjects

▶ read and understand a range of straightforward texts

▶ write a range of texts to communicate information, ideas and opinions using formats and styles suitable for their purpose and audience.

To do this you have to be able to do all of the things in the right-hand column.

Level 1 Skill standards	What you need to do
Speaking, Listening and Communication Take full part in formal and informal discussions and exchanges that include unfamiliar subjects	• Make relevant and extended contributions to discussions, allowing for and responding to others' input. • Prepare for and contribute to the formal discussion of ideas and opinions. • Make different kinds of contributions to discussions. • Present information/points of view clearly and in appropriate language.
Reading Read and understand a range of straightforward texts	• Identify the main points and ideas and how they are presented in a variety of texts. • Read and understand texts in detail. • Utilise information contained in texts. • Identify suitable responses to text. In more than one type of text.
Writing Write a range of texts to communicate information, ideas and opinions using formats and styles suitable for their purpose and audience	• Write clearly and coherently including an appropriate level of detail. • Present information in a logical sequence. • Use language, format and structure suitable for purpose and audience. • Use correct grammar including correct and consistent use of tense. • Ensure written work includes generally accurate punctuation and spelling and that meaning is clear. In more than one type of text.

Level 2

If you look at the Level 2 table below, you can see that it is set out in the same way as the Level 1 table on page vi. There is more to do for Level 2 because it's a higher qualification. If you achieve a Level 2, you will be able to:

▶ make a range of contributions to discussions in a range of contexts, including those that are unfamiliar, and make effective presentations

▶ select, read, understand and compare texts and use them to gather information, ideas, arguments and opinions

▶ write a range of texts, including extended written documents, communicating information, ideas and opinions effectively and persuasively.

As with Level 1, you will be tested on the skills listed in the right-hand column. The things you need to master require explanation and practice. This book explains what all of the words mean and how to pass the tests for Reading and Writing.

Level 2 Skill standards	What you need to do
Speaking, Listening and Communication Make a range of contributions to discussions in a wide range of contexts, and make effective presentations	• Consider complex information and give a relevant, cogent response in appropriate language. • Present information and ideas clearly and persuasively to others. • Adapt contributions to suit audience, purpose and situation. • Make significant contributions to discussions, taking a range of roles and helping to move discussion forward.
Reading Select, read, understand and compare texts and use them to gather information, ideas, arguments and opinions	• Select and use different types of texts to obtain and utilise relevant information. • Read and summarise, succinctly, information/ideas from different sources. • Identify the purposes of texts and comment on how meaning is conveyed. • Detect point of view, implicit meaning and/or bias. • Analyse texts in relation to audience needs and consider suitable responses. In three or more texts.
Writing Write a range of texts, including extended written documents, communicating information, ideas and opinions effectively and persuasively	• Present information/ideas concisely, logically and persuasively. • Present information on complex subjects clearly and concisely. • Use a range of different styles of writing for different purposes. • Use a range of sentence structures, including complex sentences, and paragraphs to organise written communication effectively. • Punctuate written text using commas, apostrophes and inverted commas accurately. • Ensure written work is fit for purpose and audience, with accurate spelling and grammar that support clear meaning. In a range of text types.

How this book works

Teaching

This book takes each and all of the bullet points in the 'What you need to do' column of the skill standards for Reading and Writing tables and explains what the words mean. For example, the first bullet point for Level 2 Reading is 'Select and use different types of texts to obtain and utilise relevant information'. In Chapter 3, 'relevant information' is explored and explained fully with examples and practice.

In Level 2 Writing, for example, the skill 'Present information/ideas concisely, logically and persuasively' is required. The words 'concisely' and 'logically' are explored and explained in the teaching section of Chapter 6 with examples and practice.

Activities

After the teaching section, you are given activities to do which will reinforce what you have learned. These are done individually or with a partner, and usually need some note-taking or discussion.

Activity 2

Match up each writing activity with a purpose.

Writing activities		Purposes	
1	Writing about what happened in a football match	A	Argue
2	Writing about how a car engine works	B	Advise
3	Writing a leaflet asking for a donation	C	Instruct
4	Writing about the different causes of homelessness	D	Review
5	Writing about how to put a flat-pack table together	E	Report
6	Writing to depict your favourite seaside place	F	Describe
7	Writing to put forward a strongly held point of view	G	Persuade
8	Writing to give details about a forthcoming event	H	Analyse
9	Writing to help people in their relationships	I	Inform
10	Writing about a film you have seen	J	Explain

Mini tests

At the end of each chapter there is a mini test, which requires you to use all the skills of reading and writing that have been presented and practised in the lessons.

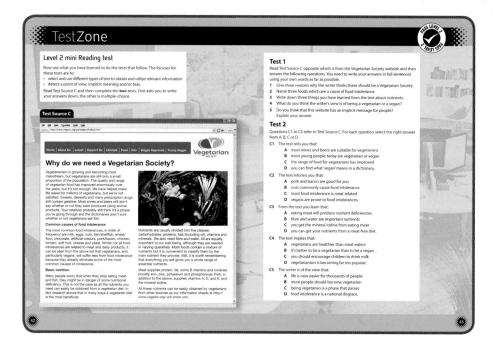

Speaking, Listening and Communication tasks

At the end of each chapter there are also suggestions for Speaking, Listening and Communication tasks, usually related to the theme or ideas used for reading or writing. You can use the tasks in class to get your Level 1 or Level 2 in Speaking, Listening and Communication because this is marked by your teacher or tutor.

Sample complete tests

At the end of the book, Chapter 8 includes complete Level 1 and Level 2 Reading and Writing tests. You can use these a bit like a mock examination. They show you what the tests will look like.

I hope you enjoy using the book and wish you every success in your Functional Skills English qualification.

David Stone

Section A Reading

Introduction to Functional Skills English: Reading

This section aims to encourage you to develop your reading skills in response to a range of functional texts. The teaching, texts and activities are all geared towards helping you become familiar with the coverate and range of the Functional Skills English test. They are also helping you become familiar with the Functional Skills English skill standard for Reading. These are the broad skills that underpin the test that you will be taking.

Peer/Self-assessment

Before starting each lesson, carefully read the skill standard opposite and the relevant 'My learning' section – you will be given the opportunity to assess how well you have done on these before and after the Reading tests. You will also have the chance to compare your test answers with some sample student work.

Test Zone

This section at the end of each chapter will provide you with a range of real and stimulating texts, plus examples, teaching and lots of activities to practise! Once you have completed this section you should be in a stronger position to take the AQA Functional English Level 2 Reading test.

Functional Skills English: Speaking, Listening and Communication

In each of the following chapters you will find suggested Speaking, Listening and Communication tasks. These tasks relate to the material in the Reading chapters. Your teacher or tutor will decide whether you will use these tasks and, if so, will also help adapt them to your needs.

Skill standards

Below are the skill standards for Levels 1 and 2, mapped to their coverage in this book.

Skill standard (Level 1)	Coverage and range	Coverage in the Student Book
Read and understand a range of straightforward texts.	• Identify the main points and ideas and how they are presented in a variety of texts. • Read and understand texts in detail. • Utilise information contained in texts. • Identify suitable responses to texts. In more than one type of text.	Pages 4–15

Skill standard (Level 2)	Coverage and range	Coverage in the Student Book
Select, read, understand and compare texts and use them to gather information, ideas, arguments and opinions.	• Select and use different types of texts to obtain and utilise relevant information.	Pages 32–47, 48–59
	• Read and summarise, succinctly, information/ideas from different sources.	Pages 18–31, 48–59
	• Identify the purposes of texts and comment on how effectively meaning is conveyed.	Pages 18–31, 48–59
	• Detect point of view, implicit meaning and/or bias	Pages 48–59
	• Analyse texts in relation to audience needs and consider suitable responses. In three or more texts.	Pages 48–59

This lesson will help you to:
● understand what 'identify' means
● understand how to identify key words and phrases.

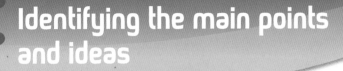

Identifying the main points and ideas

What does 'identify' mean?

The first thing you will have to do in your Level 1 Reading test is identify the main points and ideas and how they are presented.

So, what does **identify** mean? Activity 1 will help you to understand this word.

Activity 1

Choose one of the following phrases which explains what the witness of a crime has to do.

1 pick on the suspect
2 pick up the suspect
3 pick out the suspect

Key term

Identify means:

• **pick out**
• **spot**
• **recognise**

How to pick out key words and phrases

In order to identify or pick out the main points and ideas you need to be able to pick out the key words or phrases. So, what are key words? A key opens a lock – to a door or a box. A key word opens up the meaning of a piece of writing.

Now you are going to look at a sample text. Opposite are three parts of a leaflet from the charity Practical Action. You need to study them carefully to pick out the main points and ideas. Read the writing in the main part of the leaflet carefully then complete Activity 2.

Darfur is one of the driest parts of Sudan – so dry that sometimes rain falls for just two hours, in the whole year.

That's just 40mm of rain to last all year (in the UK, we get an average of 1,200mm). Families in Sudan do everything they can to grow enough food to eat, but without water, crops wither and die – and people do too, in their thousands.

But something's happening. Small banks of earth are appearing, curving across the land. And inside each curve, crops are growing, green and healthy, enough to feed a family all year round.

These earth banks are called terraces, and each forms **a crescent – a simple shape that holds onto vital water, and pushes hunger away.** You can help another family build one, with Practical Action.

Make a gift of £25 and you could pay for the tools and training a farmer needs.

The tool kit that's saving lives

This local spade, called a Kodal, is used to dig a trench...

...the soil is piled up into a crescent shape with a fork...

...and an A-frame checks that each terrace is level.

Activity 2

Find some key words and phrases in paragraphs 3 and 5. It is a good idea to make a table to collect the key words in. Copy and complete the table below. The key words and phrases for paragraphs 1, 2 and 4 have been found for you.

Paragraph	Key words
1	Darfur, driest, dry
2	without water, crops wither and die – and people do too
3	
4	terraces, crescent, holds onto vital water
5	

Whenever you come across a text you have to answer questions on, always read it through twice. The first time you will get the general idea, the second time you will notice more detail.

PASS LEVEL 1

My learning objectives ▶

This lesson will help you to:
- understand what the main points tell us
- understand why the main points have been included and how they are presented

What the main points mean and how they are presented

The tool kit that's saving lives

This local spade, called a Kodal, is used to dig a trench...

...the soil is piled up into a crescent shape with a fork...

...and an A-frame checks that each terrace is level.

The main points and why they have been included

Remind yourself of the two smaller parts of the 'Practical Action' leaflet opposite. Then complete Activity 1. This activity looks at what the 'tool kit' box and the photograph are telling us and why they have been included in the leaflet.

Activity 1

1   Copy and complete the following table. It will help you to understand what these features are telling us and why they have been included. See if you can add at least one extra point into each box.

	What is it telling us?	Why has it been included?
'Tool kit' box	• Shows you what you can buy a farmer for £25. •	• Makes some of the words and ideas into a diagram. •
Photograph	• Shows the use of one of the tools. •	• Helps you identify with the people of Sudan. •

2   Put the main points you have found from your key words table (Activity 2, page 5) and the table above into three or four full sentences. Then try to reduce these sentences into one sentence. Compare your sentence with the ones below.

Darfur in Sudan is very dry and without water, crops and people die. But curved terraces can be built which hold water to grow crops all year round. If you give £25 you can provide a farmer with the tools to build curved terraces.

If you send £25 you could help prevent people in Sudan from dying of starvation.

How the main points and ideas are presented

You need to be able to explain how these main points and ideas are **presented**.

For example, the flag of Sudan is organised as a rectangle with three horizontal stripes – red, white and black – with a green triangle on the left-hand side.

The reason for this is that red, white, black and green are called the pan-Arab colours and have been linked to the Arab people for centuries. The red stripe represents Sudan's martyrs. The white represents peace. The black represents Sudan; in Arabic 'Sudan' means black. Green represents prosperity and agriculture.

Activity 2

What is there to say about the way the 'Practical Action' leaflet (page 5) is presented? The leaflet is *arranged* in three parts:

Part 1 There is a section of writing which explains the main points of the leaflet.

Part 2 There are drawings which show us what the tool kit is.

Part 3 There is a photograph of the actual place.

What else can you say about how the writing section is presented? Look back at the leaflet and use the following headings to complete this task. (Some examples have been included for each to get you started.)

The *order* of the writing is:

about the problems in Sudan. What else?

The leaflet is *structured* to include:

the 'tool kit' box. What else?

The leaflet is *put together* using colour:

perhaps the orange/red background represents the sandy soil which grows nothing. What else?

The writing part is *shaped* like a crescent:

Why do you think that is?

My learning objectives ▶

This lesson will help you to:
● understand texts in detail
● understand what the detail in a picture tells you.

Understanding the text in detail

What does 'understanding the text in detail' mean?

You need to be able to understand the text in **detail**. When we put the main points and ideas from the last lesson down in writing, we left out lots of things such as description, explanation and persuasion. Now you are going to look deeper into the text to find the fine points. You need to look more thoroughly than before. Then you will be showing a detailed understanding.

First, look at the pictures below.

Key term

Detail means:
• more thoroughly
• fine points
• closer
• extra
• fuller
• deeper into
• minutely.

You will often need to answer questions about pictures or other illustrations. They are a kind of text. You should 'read' them in the same way: get the general picture first, then look around it more carefully.

The picture above shows a soldier talking to the queen. It is an overall view – all of the main points are there: three male figures and one female figure, a dog, the doorway, a window, furniture. The picture below is a closer, deeper look at the window in the background; we are looking at this window more thoroughly: it is a detail of the main picture.

Activity 1

1   Looking back at the 'Practical Action' leaflet (page 5), what are some of the details in the leaflet to do with rain? For example:

> 'Darfur is one of the driest parts of Sudan'; 'that's just 40mm of rain to last all year'.

Try to find two more details to do with rain.

2   Now write these details in full sentences in your own words (as far as possible). For example:

> In Darfur, one of the driest parts of Sudan, there is only 40mm of rain to last the whole year.

Notice that, in Activity 1, you should have shown good understanding of the detail by working out how much more rain there is in the UK than in Darfur.

Activity 2

Look carefully at the photograph from the leaflet. To explain in detail what you understand the photograph to be showing, you should be able to describe every part of it. You might also need to make some sensible guesses about what you see.

1   What can we say about the detail in the photograph? Below is a list of what might be seen in the photograph. Read the points and decide for each one if you agree with what is written:

   a   A man is holding an A-frame.

   b   He is explaining to a group of women what it is and how it works.

   c   The people seem interested in what the man is saying.

   d   The women are in the native dress of Sudan.

   e   There is a jeep nearby, probably belonging to the aid workers demonstrating how to use the A-frame.

2   How would you describe the land and the trees?

Remember, **detail** means *fuller, more thoroughly, extra, fine points* to be understood.

My learning objectives ▶

This lesson will help you to:
- understand what 'suitable' means
- understand what 'suitable response' means

Utilise and identify suitable responses to texts

The final thing you will be asked to do in your Level 1 Reading test is to identify **suitable** responses to texts and say how you would **utilise**, or make use of, the information.

Key terms

Suitable means:
- fitting
- right
- sensible
- apt
- relevant
- to the point
- appropriate
- proper
- applicable.

Utilise means:
- use
- make use of
- put to use.

Activity 1

We often have to act or respond in a 'suitable' way in everyday life.

1 Here are some examples of real-life situations. For each one write down, or discuss with a partner, what would be a suitable response.

   a It is Mothering Sunday – what are you going to do about it?

   b Your sister has just got engaged – what are you going to say to her fiancé?

   c Your granddad is ill – what do you say to him on the phone?

   d A friend is in trouble – how do you react when you see them?

2 Think of some recent times when you know you responded in a suitable way; write down what they were.

The leaflet we have been looking at contains another page – see page 11.

There are a number of actions you might take which would be a fitting, right and sensible response to this text. These are the ways of making use of the information in the leaflet.

You could:

▶ find out more about the problems of growing crops and staying alive in Third World countries

▶ look up the 'Practical Action' website on the Internet

▶ organise a fund-raising event in your school to raise money.

I'll help give another family the tools to beat hunger

Title   First Name
_____

Surname
_____

Address
_____

_____

                         Postcode
_____

Tel no: Email:

To help us save costs and time, if you are happy to be contacted by telephone and/or email with updates on our projects, campaigning and fundraising please provide your contact details. You can unsubscribe at any time by writing to us via Freepost at the a address below.

Here's my gift of: ☐ **£25** ☐ **£50**   **OR**

☐ **my own amount of £** _____

☐ I'd like to give by cheque/postal order/charity voucher made payable to Practical Action

   OR

☐ Please debit my Visa/MasterCard/CharityCard/Maestro (please delete as appropriate)

Credit card no. ☐☐☐☐ ☐☐☐☐ ☐☐☐☐ ☐☐☐☐ ☐☐☐

Valid from ☐☐ ☐☐   Expiry date ☐☐ ☐☐   (Maestro only) Issue no. ☐☐

Signature _____   Date ☐☐☐☐☐

If you did raise money, or wanted to send some of your own, the most suitable response you could make would be to fill in the form.

To do this you would need to understand the main points and some of the detail in the form. You would then be utilising the form for its proper purpose.

Peer/Self-assessment activity

In this chapter you have learned and practised some skills to do with being able to read and understand texts at Level 1. Before you do a short test, think about the work you have been doing and how confident you are about what you have learned. Then tick the boxes which are closest to how you feel.

Skill	Not confident	Need some more support	Very confident
I can identify the main points and ideas and how they are presented in a text.			
I can read and understand texts in detail.			
I can utilise and identify suitable responses to texts.			

Level 1 mini Reading test

Now use what you have learned to do the tests that follow.

Read Test Source A then complete the **two** tests. One asks you to write your answers down, the other is multiple-choice.

Test Source A

CAFOD
just one world

Dirty water causes more deaths in the developing world than anything else. Yet many lives could be saved using a simple water filter like the one in the drawing. CAFOD is helping to give people in the developing world clean water. With a donation from you, we can do more. Please send as much money as you can.

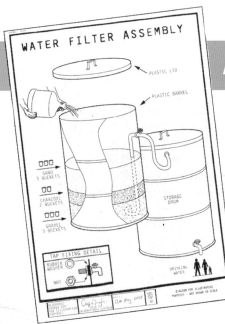

A simple filter saves hundreds of lives

It takes just ten minutes for filthy river water to filter through the sand, gravel and charcoal and come out sparkling clean and safe to drink. Local people are trained to check on the bacteria levels in the water and clean the filter regularly to keep it working effectively.

"*When we drink the filtered water our bodies feel fine* "
Sunday Pam, Nigeria

Safe, filtered water prevents diarrhoea – the biggest cause of death for children in the developing world

Test 1

Read Test Source A opposite and then answer the following questions. You need to write your answers in full sentences using your own words as far as possible.

1 What is the main point being made in the leaflet?
2 How is the leaflet organised and presented?
3 How does the water filter work?
4 Explain what the photograph is showing.
5 What does the writer of the leaflet want you to do?

Test 2

Questions A1 to A5 refer to Test Source A. For each question select the right answer from A, B, C or D.

A1 The main purpose of the leaflet is to:
- **A** explain how a water filter is assembled
- **B** persuade you to give money to CAFOD
- **C** warn that drinking dirty water is dangerous
- **D** inform you about conditions in the Third World.

A2 One of the main ideas in the leaflet is that:
- **A** a water filter is able to save many lives
- **B** the water filter is difficult to assemble
- **C** we are lucky to have clean water in the UK
- **D** clean water will cure diarrhoea.

A3 The photograph is effective because:
- **A** it shows a mother taking care of her children
- **B** it shows how simple the water filter is
- **C** it shows a typical Nigerian family scene
- **D** it shows how good filtered water is.

A4 The leaflet tells you that:
- **A** the water filter takes a long time to assemble
- **B** the filter cannot be used with filthy water
- **C** local people help to keep the filter clean
- **D** the water filter is good value for money.

A5 What does the writer of the leaflet want you to do now?
- **A** send in your own design for a water filter
- **B** raise money and send a donation to CAFOD
- **C** find out about living conditions in Nigeria
- **D** start a campaign for clean water in your school.

TestZone

Student sample answers

Here are three student responses to Test 1 on the CAFOD text (page 12). First, remind yourself of the text and the questions on pages 12–13. Then read the answers below together with the examiner comments around and after the answers.

Student A Pass ✓

1 The point being made is that dirty water kills more people than any other illness. ✓

> One valid point made from three in the mark scheme.

2 The leaflet is organised to show a diagram of a water filter, ✓ a section telling you about the filter and about the people who check the levels of bacteria, ✓ and speech telling you how the filter has improved the water ✓ with a picture below showing children drinking the water, ✓ and is presented well, put into sections ✓ which also persuades you to give money.

> Five points are made in a full and focused answer, maximum marks are awarded.

3 The filter works by the water being filtered through sand, gravel and charcoal. ✓

> There are three points in the mark scheme, one of which is made.

4 The photograph shows young people ✓ drinking the clean water. ✓

> Two valid points are made.

5 The writer wants you to help with the filters, ✓ by giving them a donation, ✓ so all the children will have safe water that they can drink.

> A full answer gaining maximum marks.

Examiner comment

The student showed a good understanding of the leaflet and focused well on the questions. Marks were dropped because in one or two cases, particularly question 3, further points of detail could have been made. A mark of 10/15 would achieve Level 1.

Student B *Borderline* ✓✗

1 The main point that is being made in the leaflet is that filtered water will stop so many people from dying ✓ and that you should send money to help. ✓

> Two valid points being made. The main points are really about the developing world.

2 It is presented by having important information in a box with a bold title ✓ and has pictures ✓ to help people understand.

> Two points about the organisation and presentation are made, there are more in the mark scheme.

3 The water filter works by letting dirty water filter through sand, gravel and charcoal ✓ for ten minutes. ✓

> Two valid points are made in the answer.

4 The photograph on the right is showing a small child drinking water from a bowl. ✗

> There is no mention of the fact that the drinking water is clean because of the filter which is the point of the picture.

5 The writer of the leaflet wants you to send as much money as possible to CAFOD ✓ to help fund the filters. ✓

> A focused answer gaining full marks.

Examiner comment

A good understanding of the leaflet but marks were lost because there is more detail to report for question 2 and the answer to question 4 missed the point. A mark of 8/15 is a borderline mark which would probably achieve Level 1.

TestZone

Student C Fail ✗

1 It is trying to stress the importance of clean water. ✗

> This is a very general answer which mentions neither 'deaths', 'developing world' nor 'water filter' and so receives no marks.

2 It is organised in a simple format with clear fonts and images. ✓

> This just about earns one mark. The format is not, in fact, simple; the text is clear but there is no detail about the images.

3 The water is filtered through sand, gravel and charcoal. ✓

> This is one point made of the three available in the mark scheme.

4 The photograph is showing children drinking filtered ✓ water and how important it is.

> The first point is correct, the second point is general and rather vague.

5 Understand the importance of filtered water and make a donation towards CAFOD. ✓

> The main point is made for one mark.

Examiner comment

The student's responses are rather vague and general in places, particularly questions 1 and 2 which say very little of substance about the leaflet. The mark scheme indicates that there is more focus and detail needed in response to the questions. The mark of 4/15 would not achieve Level 1.

Peer/Self-assessment activity

With a partner, read the three student answers on pages 14, 15 and above noting the comments made by the examiner. Then read each other's answers to test 1 on page 13.

1 Compare the answers you and your partner wrote with the answers from Student A. Did you do as well? If not, what did you miss?

2 Can you find at least four effective ways the leaflet is presented including some interesting design features? Discuss with your partner what is meant by 'design features'.

3 Look carefully at the photograph again. Imagine you are the photographer and that you are actually there. Now discuss with your partner and write down everything that the photograph is showing the reader. There's quite a lot going on even though it's a small photograph.

4 What do you think Student B needed to do to make sure of getting Level 1 instead of being borderline?

5 Discuss with your partner why you think Student C was awarded no marks for question 1 and only one mark for question 2.
▶ How did you do on those questions?
▶ What did you miss?

You need to be focused on the text and the question and detailed in your answers. Discuss with your partner what these words mean.

6 Discuss with your partner what each of you needs to do to improve your marks next time.

Skill standard

Take full part in formal and informal discussions and exchanges that include unfamiliar subjects.

What you need to do:

▶ Make relevant and extended contributions to discussions, allowing for and responding to others' input.

▶ Prepare for and contribute to the formal discussion of ideas and opinions.

▶ Make different kinds of contributions to discussions.

▶ Present information/points of view clearly and in appropriate language.

Your teacher or tutor will help you to decide whether to use the following tasks. They will also help you to organise the tasks should you attempt them.

Task 1: Discussion

Discuss, in a group, some of the problems and challenges facing young people of your age in Third World countries like Nigeria.

You will need to find out about:

▶ family life

▶ challenges about food and drink

▶ school life

▶ what they do for leisure and fun.

The CAFOD website will give you some ideas: www.cafod.org.uk.

Task 2: Discussion

Read the CAFOD leaflet in your group and visit the website where it tells you about donations.

Discuss ideas for raising money by getting people to sponsor you.

My learning ▶

This lesson will help you to:
● understand the audience of a text
● understand the purpose of a text.

Audience and purpose

Audience

To understand a text and what the writer had in mind when he or she wrote it, we need to think about the audience or readers the text was written for.

The word audience literally means 'hearing', and we meet the word 'audio' a lot in everyday life. Audiences come in different shapes and sizes; an audience can be one person, or in the case of a music festival several hundred thousand.

An audience is made up of the people who experience what is going on: the watchers, listeners and readers. Writers have an audience in mind when they write their text. For example, we could say that the audience of a television guide is made up of:

▶ people who want to know what time television programmes are on

▶ people who are interested in reading behind-the-scenes stories of television programmes.

Here is a listening audience

Here is a reading audience

Here is a watching audience

Activity 1

1 Write down the last time you were part of an audience.

2 Write down how many different sorts of audience you can think of.

3 Think of two or three written texts such as specific newspapers or magazines, novels, websites or even textbooks! Jot down the audience or audiences that might find these interesting.

Purpose

Having a clear purpose in mind is important. For example, a mountain rescue team is clear and focused in its purpose to find and help people in trouble.

Different purposes

Knowing the purpose – the aim – of a task is important and it's the same when you read what people write. When people write things for you to read, they have a purpose in mind.

Here are some examples which you will meet in Functional English at Level 2. The writer's purpose might be to:

report	instruct	persuade	review	advise
explain	describe	argue	analyse	inform.

You will need to identify the main purpose behind a piece of writing by asking yourself:

What was the main thing on the writer's mind when they wrote this?

Watch out – sometimes people write with more than one purpose in mind!

Activity 2

Match up each writing activity with a purpose.

Writing activities	Purposes	
1 Writing about what happened in a football match	A	Argue
2 Writing about how a car engine works	B	Advise
3 Writing a leaflet asking for a donation	C	Instruct
4 Writing about the different causes of homelessness	D	Review
5 Writing about how to put a flat-pack table together	E	Report
6 Writing to depict your favourite seaside place	F	Describe
7 Writing to put forward a strongly held point of view	G	Persuade
8 Writing to give details about a forthcoming event	H	Analyse
9 Writing to help people in their relationships	I	Inform
10 Writing about a film you have seen	J	Explain

Purposes and pictures

Purposes

You are about to look at a sample text on careers.

The audiences for this text are:

▶ people who are interested in catering

▶ people who want a goal or ambition to work towards.

You need to work out what the purpose of the text is, and the purpose of the pictures. Read the text carefully a couple of times then complete Activities 1 and 2 (page 21).

○ ○ ○

◀ ▶ | C | + | http://careersforyou.com | Q▾

Careers for you

▶ Careers Advice Home

▶ Start Here

▶ In Your Region

▶ Find A Course

▶ Career Tools

▶ Jobs and Careers

▶ Help and Advice

▶ Podcasts

▶ Other Languages

▶ Get In Touch

▶ Discussion Forums

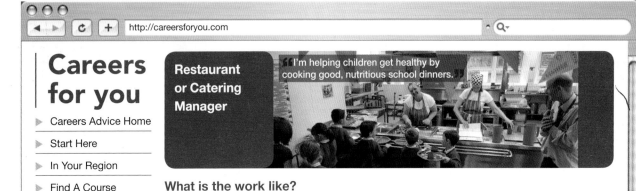

Restaurant or Catering Manager

I'm helping children get healthy by cooking good, nutritious school dinners.

What is the work like?

Restaurant and catering managers are responsible for making sure customers are satisfied with the quality of food and service provided in a range of eating places.

As a restaurant manager, you could work in catering outlets such as: hotels, small independent restaurants, eateries that are part of a large chain, and fast-food outlets. You would be front-of-house, welcoming customers to the restaurant and showing them to their table.

As a catering manager you would work in larger catering operations, such as business or factory canteens, hospitals or schools. You would have less contact with customers than a restaurant manager, and spend more time behind the scenes.

Your duties as a restaurant or catering manager would include:

- planning healthy, nutritious menus
- ensuring good, efficient service to customers
- running the business in line with strict hygiene, health and safety guidelines
- ensuring a high standard of service and presentation

- making sure all staff are fully trained
- keeping staff motivated
- organising shift patterns and rotas
- managing stock control and budgets
- advertising vacancies and recruiting staff.

What qualifications and experience will employers look for?

To apply for a trainee manager post, you will usually need a good general standard of education plus relevant experience.

Another way you could get into a management position would be to work your way up. For example, you could start as a waiter/waitress and with experience and qualifications (such as an NVQ Level 3 in Food Service Advanced Craft), you could take on more responsibilities, supervising less-experienced colleagues. You would then be in a good position to apply for a trainee management post.

Many hotel chains run management trainee schemes that can lead to restaurant or catering management and some employers will accept you with A-levels or a BTEC National award. Fast-food chains, catering companies and large restaurants may also run management trainee schemes.

Now look at the list of purposes on the right. It is possible to go through the list to find the purpose of the text.

▶ The text opposite is not REPORTING on a day in the life of a Restaurant or Catering Manager.

▶ It's not trying to INSTRUCT you to be a Restaurant or Catering Manager.

▶ It's not trying to PERSUADE you to become a Restaurant or Catering Manager.

▶ This text is EXPLAINING:

　▶ what a Restaurant or Catering Manager is responsible for

　▶ what kinds of places they work in.

Purposes
Report
Instruct
Persuade
Comment
Advise
Describe
Analyse
Review
Explain
Argue
Inform

Activity 1

1　Write down at least three more things the text is explaining about the job of Restaurant or Catering Manager.

2　Sometimes a text seems to have more than one purpose. Write down, from the boxed list, what other purpose you think the text fulfils as well as to explain.

The importance of pictures

Now you need to think about the use of pictures, because pictures can be part of a text. What purpose do you think the pictures in the 'Careers for you' text have?

Look at the pictures carefully. One shows a woman in a school canteen serving food. There is a caption to this picture which is also part of the text. The other shows a place setting in what looks like a very smart restaurant. If you read the main text again you'll see that the pictures connect to parts of the writing.

For the Reading test, you will need to be clear about the writer's purpose. When you are doing the Writing test, you will need to be clear about your purpose. Try to memorise the list of purposes in this lesson.

Activity 2

1　Write down how you think the pictures in the 'Careers for you' text relate to the writing.

2　Identify exactly which parts of the writing link to each picture.

3　Say why you think the pictures help you as a reader.

This lesson will help you to:
- comment on how meaning is conveyed.

Commenting on how meaning is conveyed

Conveying meaning effectively

Look carefully at the text below from a leaflet about homeless children in South America. It **conveys** its meaning very effectively by the way it's presented as well as the words which have been used.

Key term

Convey means:
- communicate
- make known
- reveal
- make the point.

Hundreds of children live on the streets

With your help, they won't die there

<u>For thousands of children in Colombia's capital city, Bogotá, every day is a fight for survival.</u>

- They have no homes, no families and no way out.

These youngsters live on the streets, scratching around in rubbish bins or begging for food and sleeping in discarded storage bags.

- They are constantly frightened of being <u>attacked</u>, <u>kidnapped</u> or simply <u>starving to death</u>.

But there is hope. Our YMCA centre has given many children <u>safe new lives</u>, far away from the dangerous and violent streets of Bogotá.

The leaflet on page 22 conveys its meaning **effectively**.

Activity 1

With a partner, discuss and write down the ways you think the writer has made the presentation of this leaflet effective.

Some things you ought to consider include:

- the layout – how the paragraphs are placed
- the use of colour – black, red and then green
- how certain words and ideas are made to stand out
- the pictures – are they real photographs?

Effective use of language

Now you need to look carefully at the language the writer has used, not just to understand the facts but to consider how the words affect us: how they are effective.

There are ways of describing or explaining how writers express themselves to make their language effective. Here are some:

informal	complex	personal	clear	formal
emotive	focused	shocking	determined	humorous
confused	detached	serious	factual	detailed.

Activity 2

1   In pairs, discuss which of the words above best describe the way the writer of the article 'Hundreds of children live on the streets' has expressed him/herself.

2   Why do you think he/she chose to write in this way?

Now you've seen how presentation and language can convey meaning effectively in this text, look again at the 'Careers for you' article on page 20.

3   Discuss and write down how the writer of 'Careers for you' has used presentation and language to convey the meaning of his/her text effectively.

My learning objectives ▶

This lesson will help you to:
● summarise information and ideas
● summarise succinctly.

Reading and summarising

Summarise succinctly

Here are two examples which **summarise succinctly**.

A On the back of an edition of Shakespeare's play *Romeo and Juliet*, you are given an outline of the story, such as:

The tragic tale of the passion of two young lovers whose lives were destroyed by a family feud.

B This weather forecast gives the main points about the weather coming up. Weather forecasters call this a synopsis.

Weather forecast

Tonight the north of England will be clear but cold with the possibility of ground frost. Any morning mist will soon clear to give a sunny, warm day with temperatures as high as 20 degrees Celsius.

A summary will be brief and will leave out needless details. But it must include the main points. In other words, a summary needs to be 'succinct'.

Key terms

Summarise means:

• give the main points
• give a run-down
• outline
• review
• sum up
• make a synopsis
• put in a nutshell.

Succinctly means:

• in a few, well-chosen words
• briefly
• concisely
• condensed
• to the point.

Activity 1

1 Write down places and times when you have read or written something that was a summary.

2 Look again at the 'Careers for you' text on page 20. Try to find the main points. You can do this by copying and completing this table. Fill in the key words or phrases for paragraphs 3, 5 and 6.

Paragraph	Key words referring to Restaurant or Catering Manager
1	responsible, customers, satisfied
2	catering outlets, hotels, welcoming customers
3	
4	duties, planning, high standard, organising, managing
5	
6	
7	hotel chains, trainee schemes, A-levels, BTEC

PASS LEVEL 2 ✔

Get used to the idea of seeing a large piece of text as a series of paragraphs. Each paragraph will have a 'topic' or main sentence – usually the first one, but maybe the last. To understand the text quickly, focus on what the topic sentence says.

Activity 2 below turns the key words from Activity 1 into sentences, as the examples show. This will help you to create a first draft of your summary.

Activity 2

Write sentences about paragraphs 2, 4 and 6 of the text on page 20.

1 As a Restaurant or Catering Manager you are responsible for keeping customers satisfied.

2 _____

3 In larger operations you'd be behind the scenes.

4 _____

5 To become a manager you need a good general education and experience.

6 _____

7 Some hotels run training schemes for people with A-levels or a BTEC.

Being more succinct

We now need to make this more succinct. The first four sentences are about the job and the last three are about what you need to get the job. So we could write the following:

▶ A Restaurant or Catering Manager is responsible for planning, organising and managing to a high standard, whether in small outlets welcoming customers, or larger outlets working behind the scenes.

▶ With a good general education and some experience you can join a trainee course, some of which are run by large organisations.

A one-sentence summary might look like this:

▶ Starting with a good general education, a successful trainee can become a Restaurant or Catering Manager responsible for managing a variety of outlets to a high standard.

Activity 3

1 Following the advice and practice in summarising, write two sentences which sum up the message in the text on page 22.

2 Now put all the information and persuasion into one, succinct sentence.

Peer/Self-assessment activity

In this chapter you have learned and practised some skills to do with being able to read and understand texts at Level 2. Before you do a short test, think about the work you have been doing and how confident you are about what you have learned. Then tick the boxes which are closest to how you feel.

Skill	Not confident	Need some more support	Very confident
I can understand the audience and purpose of a text.			
I can see how the meaning of a text is effectively conveyed.			
I can summarise, succinctly, information and ideas.			

TestZone

Level 2 mini Reading test

Now use what you have learned to do the test that follows. The focuses for this test are to:
- read and summarise, succinctly, information/ideas
- identify the purposes of texts and comment on how effectively meaning is conveyed.

Read Test Source B and then complete the **two** tests. One asks you to write down your answers, the other is multiple-choice.

Test Source B

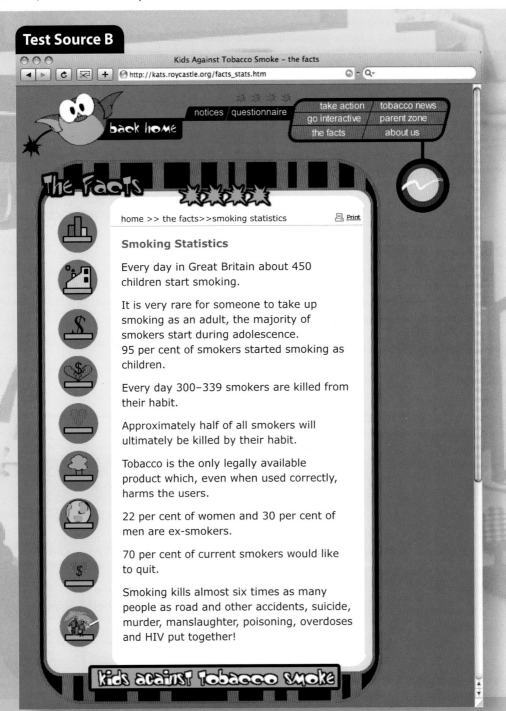

Kids Against Tobacco Smoke – the facts

http://kats.roycastle.org/facts_stats.htm

notices / questionnaire

take action | tobacco news
go interactive | parent zone
the facts | about us

back home

The Facts

home >> the facts>>smoking statistics   Print

Smoking Statistics

Every day in Great Britain about 450 children start smoking.

It is very rare for someone to take up smoking as an adult, the majority of smokers start during adolescence.
95 per cent of smokers started smoking as children.

Every day 300–339 smokers are killed from their habit.

Approximately half of all smokers will ultimately be killed by their habit.

Tobacco is the only legally available product which, even when used correctly, harms the users.

22 per cent of women and 30 per cent of men are ex-smokers.

70 per cent of current smokers would like to quit.

Smoking kills almost six times as many people as road and other accidents, suicide, murder, manslaughter, poisoning, overdoses and HIV put together!

Kids against Tobacco smoke

Test 1

Read Test Source B which is part of the 'Kids Against Tobacco Smoke' website and then answer the following questions. You need to write your answers in full sentences using your own words as far as possible.

1   Write two full sentences which summarise the information in the web page.
2   What do you think is the purpose of the web page?
3   Who do you think the writer had in mind when the web page was written?
4   Write down why the use of statistics in the web page is effective.
5   In what ways do you think the web page is effectively presented?

Test 2

Questions B1 to B5 refer to Test Source B. For each question select the right answer from A, B, C or D.

B1   The main purpose of the web page is to:
   A   advertise the KATS online campaign
   B   provide facts and figures about smoking
   C   persuade adult smokers to kick the habit
   D   discourage children from starting to smoke.

B2   The main point being made in the web page is that:
   A   300 smokers will die through smoking
   B   Great Britain has the most smokers
   C   smoking is harmful and will kill you
   D   smoking cigarettes is not against the law.

B3   The web page tells you that:
   A   20 per cent of women and 32 per cent of men smoke
   B   most people started smoking as an adult
   C   most people who smoke want to stop
   D   67 per cent of smokers have successfully quit.

B4   The colourful presentation of the web page is effective because:
   A   it makes it less boring to read
   B   colour is cheaper on the Internet
   C   it helps you navigate the website
   D   it will appeal to younger readers.

B5   The text uses lots of statistics because:
   A   statistics help to make a point convincing
   B   facts and figures can be used to fool people
   C   figures are easier to read than lots of words
   D   statistics always appeal to people's emotions.

Student sample answers

Here are three student responses to Test 1 on the smoking text (page 26). Read the answers together with the examiner comments around and after them. First, remind yourself of the text and the questions (pages 26–27).

Student A *Pass* ✓

1 When you are a teenager you are more likely to become a smoker, ✓ 450 children start smoking every day. ✓ 70 per cent of smokers would like to quit ✓ because everyday 300–339 people die because of smoking. ✓

> A summary is presented in two sentences as required; the summary makes four key points clearly.

2 The purpose of the web page is to inform ✓ people/children about smoking, so hopefully they don't start. ✓

> The two points clearly made exactly reflect the mark scheme.

3 I think the web page is based on children reading it ✓ who hopefully will not start smoking.

> The correct answer is clearly given.

4 The statistics are effective because they give a number to the facts. ✓ I know that a lot of children start smoking everyday but I didn't know it was 450!

> The response is worth one point because it indicates an understanding of the focus of the question: the effect of statistics on the reader.

5 The web page is effective because it is spaced out ✓ so each point is clear. ✓ It's colourful ✓ and the KATS logo is at the bottom. ✓

> A clear and appropriate response to the question giving four valid points.

Examiner comment

The student has understood the text and its intended effects. The questions have been read carefully and addressed correctly and in detail. The mark of 12/15 would achieve Level 2.

Student B *Borderline* ✓✗

1 Smoking causes more deaths than other illnesses put together. ✓ Yet around 450 children a day start smoking. ✓

2 I think the purpose of this web page is to try and convince children to not smoke ✓

3 I think the writer had children and teenagers in mind when the web page was written. ✓

4 The use of statistics is effective because it gives the web page a more effective argument ✓ as to why smoking is bad.

5 The web page is presented effectively because of the colour ✓ and the amount of writing that has been written. ✓

A summary is presented. However, only two of the six key points in the mark scheme are made.

This secondary purpose gets a mark; the main purpose of the web page is to inform.

The correct answer is clearly given.

The student understands the focus of the question and gets the sense of the ideas expressed in the mark scheme, so is awarded one mark.

The first point is valid, the second is not developed but the idea is present; two points out of the list in the mark scheme.

Examiner comment

The student clearly understands the text and its effect. More marks could have been gained by presenting a fuller, more detailed summary in question 1 and more detail in question 5. The mark of 7/15 is borderline Level 2.

TestZone

Student C Fail ✗

1 The web page gives the reader all the facts of the consequences of smoking. Also, it gives the average percentage of all the deaths from or people that would like to quit. ✗

> The student has not presented a summary; a summary is a condensed version of the text. The response is not a version but a description of the contents of the text.

2 I think that the purpose of this web page is to enlighten ✓ people on the dangers of smoking.

> The word 'enlighten' implies 'inform' and so one mark is awarded.

3 I think that the writer had in mind all the people that had died from smoking habits. ✗

> The answer is incorrect; the web page is for 'Kids'.

4 The reason the use of statistics is useful here is because it shows that these are facts and not just stories. ✓

> An appropriate answer.

5 The web page is clear to read, ✓ uses short sentences ✓ and has catchy colours. ✓

> Three clear and appropriate responses made.

Examiner comment

The student did not respond to question 1 in an appropriate way and so lost a potential six marks. Although some aspects of the text were understood, the responses, in relation to the skills being tested, were less than successful. The mark of 5/15 would not achieve Level 2.

Peer/Self-assessment activity

With a partner, read the three student answers on pages 28, 29 and above noting the comments made by the examiner. Then read each other's answers to test 1 on page 27.

1 Compare the answers you and your partner wrote with the answers from Student A.
   ▶ Are your answers as full and detailed for questions 1 and 5?
   ▶ How many more points could you now make in response to these questions?
2 Notice the detail Student A offered for question 5.
   ▶ What did you miss from this question?
3 What should Student C have done to make sure of passing? Look carefully at where he lost marks?
4 Student C's answer to question 1 is full but a cross was given with no marks. Discuss why no marks were given.
   ▶ What went wrong in question 3 for Student C?

   ▶ What do you and your partner learn about reading Student C's failed answers?
5 Look carefully at each other's answers. How could they have been improved?

In the future...
The texts used in the test are easy to find:
   ▶ advertisements
   ▶ holiday brochures
   ▶ leaflets that come through the door
   ▶ websites on subjects that interest you.

Bring some into class and practise asking questions about what they really say and how they are put together.

Skill standard

Make a range of contributions to discussions in a range of contexts, including those that are unfamiliar, and make effective presentations.

What you need to do:

▶ Consider complex information and give a relevant, cogent response in appropriate language.

▶ Present information and ideas clearly and persuasively to others.

▶ Adapt contributions to suit audience, purpose and situation.

▶ Make significant contributions to discussions, taking a range of roles and helping to move discussion forward.

Your teacher or tutor will help you to decide whether to use the following tasks. They will also help you to organise the tasks should you attempt them.

Task 1: Discussion

Discuss the issue of homelessness among young people in Britain today. You might want to focus on a large town or city near to where your school or college is situated.

You will need to divide up the research task between the members of your group.

Here are some areas for research and discussion:

▶ Statistics which show the extent of the issue.

▶ Reasons for homelessness.

▶ Who looks after young people who are homeless?

▶ What local authority provision is there for homeless young people?

▶ What can be done to reduce the problem?

It might even be possible to do some one-to-one research with young people who are in this situation.

Task 2: Presentation

Prepare a presentation for a group of students which proposes:

Either

that cigarette advertising and selling tobacco products should be banned because of the health risks and costs.

Or

that smoking is legal and the smoking ban and propaganda against smoking is against our right to act as we wish in a free society.

This lesson will help you to:
- understand what the word 'relevant' means
- select and use relevant information from a text.

Relevant information in written and visual texts

Relevant information

Here are some pictures to illustrate what relevant means. The first is a photograph from a website advertising a company called Relevant Marketing; the second is a cartoon.

Key term

Relevant means:

- apt
- fitting
- to the point
- appropriate
- proper
- related
- selected
- suited
- sifted
- the right time and place
- to do with...

"Have you any other references apart from your mother's."

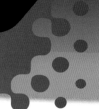

To pass your Level 2 test, you need to be able to identify the key words in a question and keep focused on them as you read the text.

Activity 1

You can work alone or with a partner for this activity. Discuss or write down your ideas on the following points:

- Look at the definitions of the word 'relevant' and add some of your own.
- Why do you think the photograph is good for advertising the company?
- How is the meaning of the word 'relevant' explored in an amusing way in the cartoon?

Read the efestivals text on page 33, which is the sort of text you are likely to face in your test. Then complete Activities 2 and 3 on page 34.

FESTIVALS | SHOP | INFORMATION | COMMUNITY | ABOUT

home >> festivals >> Glastonbury Festival

GLASTONBURY FESTIVAL INFORMATION

▼ What is Glastonbury Festival?

Glastonbury Festival is the UK's largest music festival – it's a one-off! What makes it so special is the vibe – vibrant, but mellow.

First you have the setting – 700 acres in a beautiful valley in Somerset. The site is HUGE – about a mile and a half across and a perimeter fence of about 8.5 miles. Everything is within the fence – camping and entertainment – unlike other festivals there is no arena to queue up for and enter each day.

Then you have the people – these are what makes this festival special. Like all festivals, the more you put in yourself, the better time you'll have – try not to be a passive visitor expecting to be just entertained. Interact, even if it's just by displaying an up-for-it attitude and a huge smile, explore the whole site and check out at least one show at every venue.

Along with the 100,000-plus paying ticket holders, there are around 35,000 staff and performers. The enthusiasm is such that the Kidz Field Crew are issued with written instructions saying 'if in doubt, SMILE' – a good plan for a great time.

Then you have the music, theatre, circus, cabaret, Kidz Field, shopping in the vast markets of over 700 stalls with their fantastic variety of clothes, crafts and food … and so much more – you really need to be there and experience it.

At Glastonbury Festival you'll have the time of your life! And the festival aims to raise money and awareness for good causes too.

▼ Getting In

Of course you need a ticket, which must be bought in advance. If travelling by car, you also need a parking ticket. Tickets are not available at the gates.

▼ Camping

Wherever you camp, you will end up with a VERY near neighbour.

Stewards will direct people away from full camping fields to those with space – this is for the safety of everyone. Please respect their directions – when a field is full, it's full!

Pick your spot carefully – try not to camp near the tracks or roads, and choose the higher ground if you can – this will help you stay dry.

Relevance in a written text

The text is providing information about the Glastonbury Festival. There is a lot of information in the text. Your task as the reader (the audience) is to *sift* through the text to find the information which is *fitting* and *appropriate* to your own purpose.

Imagine that you are 17 years old and you are thinking of going to Glastonbury with a friend next year for the first time. You need to find the relevant information from the text to help you. To start with we will construct a key-word table for the whole text.

Activity 2

Having read the Glastonbury Festival text, copy and complete the table below. You will need to find the key words and phrases for paragraphs 4, 5, 8 and 10.

Paragraph	Key words and phrases
1	UK's largest music festival, one-off, special vibe
2	700 acres, HUGE, fence 8 ½ miles, no queuing
3	passive/interactive, smile, check out one show every venue
4	
5	
6	time of your life, raise money, good causes
7	ticket in advance, car park, no tickets at gates
8	
9	stewards, safety, respect, fields
10	

The key-word table is a good way for you to understand what is in the text. Some of the information in the text may not be relevant to your purpose of planning to go to Glastonbury. It might be interesting information but not directly relevant.

Activity 3

1   With a partner, discuss the information from the text which you need to know if planning to go to Glastonbury. Here are some questions to ask yourselves:

a   Do you need to know about Glastonbury's 'special vibe'?

b   Do you need to know the size of the site and the fence?

c   Is the fact that there is no queuing relevant to your planning?

d   Is the advice in paragraph 3 to the point?

e   Do you need to know about the 'Kidz Field'?

f   Is the list of things to do at Glastonbury in paragraph 5 related to your planning?

g   Is the 'Getting In' information relevant?

h   How much of the 'Camping' information is appropriate to your needs?

i   Don't forget that a picture is also a text!

2   Now make a list from the text of the relevant information which fits your purpose.

Relevance in a visual text

Below is a different kind of text from which you can select some relevant information. Texts like graphs, tables, pie charts and bar charts are everyday sources of information found in newspapers and magazines. This bar chart was published on the BBC News website. This is not a very complicated chart but, like the text on page 33, it has lots of information.

Imagine you are asked this question:

Using the bar chart, what is the total turnover in €millions earned by the English clubs?

To answer this question you do not need all the information the bar chart holds. You would need to find only the relevant information from the chart. You would need to sift through the information, selecting only what you needed.

> PASS LEVEL 2
>
> To pass your Level 2 test, you need to be able to know how to read visual texts like graphs. The next time you see one in a book, newspaper or magazine, take some time to study it.

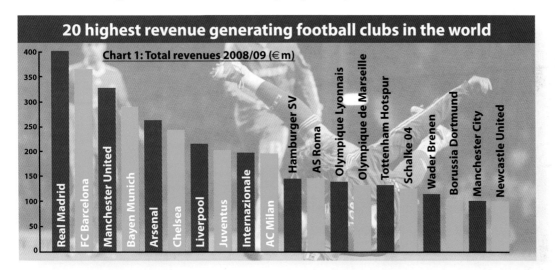

20 highest revenue generating football clubs in the world

Chart 1: Total revenues 2008/09 (€m)

Activity 4

Look carefully at the bar chart and answer the following questions about what it tells you.

Note: 'total revenues' means the total amount of money earned in a year.

1 Which is the richest football club in the world?
2 Which is the fourth richest?
3 What is Arsenal's total revenue in millions of euros?
4 What is Roma's total revenue?
5 Does AC Milan earn more money than Liverpool?
6 How much more money does Internazionale earn than Borussia Dortmund?
7 How many English clubs are there in the top 20?

Activity 5

1 Write down the steps you would take to answer the question: Using the bar chart, what is the total turnover in €millions earned by the English clubs?
2 What is the answer to the question?

Understanding the key words

The following key words may appear in the test questions. You need to know what they mean.

▶ The word 'detect' tells you that you will need to *look carefully, hunt for or decipher* something.

▶ The phrase 'point of view' indicates that there is an opinion being expressed.

▶ 'Implicit meaning' means something other than the main meaning of the text, something *implied, suggested, hidden,* or *beneath the surface.*

▶ The word 'bias' means *partial to, prejudiced about, in favour of,* or *inclined towards* or *against.* If you are a vegetarian you will be 'biased' in your view about eating meat (you will be against eating meat).

Many texts just present information without implying anything else, without presenting a point of view and without bias.

The Glastonbury Festival information text contains information relevant to planning a visit as you saw above. But it also contains much more.

Activity 1

Re-read the first three paragraphs of the Glastonbury Festival information text, printed again below. What do you think is the writer's purpose in choosing the underlined words and phrases?

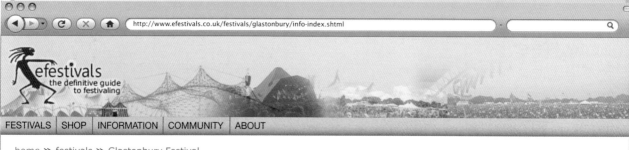

http://www.efestivals.co.uk/festivals/glastonbury/info-index.shtml

efestivals
the definitive guide
to festivaling

FESTIVALS | SHOP | INFORMATION | COMMUNITY | ABOUT

home » festivals » Glastonbury Festival

GLASTONBURY FESTIVAL INFORMATION

▼ What is Glastonbury Festival?

Glastonbury Festival is the UK's largest music festival – <u>it's a one-off!</u> What makes it <u>so special</u> is the vibe – vibrant, but mellow.

First you have the setting – 700 acres in a <u>beautiful</u> valley in Somerset. The site is HUGE – about a mile and a half across and a perimeter fence of about 8.5 miles. Everything is within the fence – camping and entertainment – <u>unlike other festivals</u> there is no arena to queue up for and enter each day.

Then you have the people – <u>these are what makes this festival special</u>. Like all festivals, <u>the more you put in yourself, the better time you'll have</u> – try not to be a passive visitor expecting to be just entertained. <u>Interact</u>, even if it's just by displaying an <u>up-for-it attitude and a huge smile</u>, explore the whole site and check out at least one show at every venue.

The purpose of the selected words in Activity 1 is more than to inform.

▶ They express the *point of view* that the Glastonbury festival is: 'a one-off', 'special', set in a place that is 'beautiful'.

▶ They *imply* that this festival is better than some others because 'it's a one-off' and you 'don't have to queue', so the text is *biased*.

▶ They *imply* that you should behave in a certain way if you go to the festival – you should 'have an input', 'show an up-for-it attitude' and 'smile'.

So the writer is doing more than giving you *relevant information* in this text – if you are able to detect it.

Activity 2

Re-read the three paragraphs below from the Glastonbury Festival information text, then complete the two tasks.

1   Write down the words and phrases where you think you can detect a point of view, implicit meaning and/or bias.

2   In each case, write a few words which explain what you think the writer's purpose is in using these words and phrases.

> Along with the 100,000-plus paying ticket holders, there are around 35,000 staff and performers. The enthusiasm is such that the Kidz Field Crew are issued with written instructions saying 'if in doubt, SMILE' – a good plan for a great time.
>
> Then you have the music, theatre, circus, cabaret, Kidz Field, shopping in the vast markets of over 700 stalls with their fantastic variety of clothes, crafts and food … and so much more – you really need to be there and experience it.
>
> At Glastonbury Festival you'll have the time of your life! And the festival aims to raise money and awareness for good causes too.

Newspapers often publish articles on issues presenting opposing points of view and bias which will interest their readers. On the following page is one on the use of real fur in the fashion industry. Read it carefully, then complete Activity 3. Discuss the questions in the activity with a partner and jot down your ideas.

Activity 3

There are two very different points of view presented here.

1 Who are the groups of people who hold the different views?
2 Summarise the view they each hold.
3 Why is Mark Townsend biased in favour of using furs?
4 Why is the PETA director biased against using furs?

THE TIMES

FUR COMPANIES LURE DESIGNERS…

Fur companies are offering sponsorship deals and expensive trips to British designers in an attempt to break the taboo on fur, an investigation by *The Times* has found.

After a ban on fur farming in Britain and successful campaigns by anti-fur groups, designers have been reluctant to promote ranges in this country for fear of retaliation. Now it has emerged that the large companies are providing expensive furs free to British designers as well as entertaining designers and stylists at their Scandinavian headquarters.

A young British designer, who wished to remain anonymous, said: 'Designers are approached by the fur companies. They offer you a trip to their fur centre in the country, it's a nice holiday and you don't have to pay for anything.'

Mark Townsend, a spokesman for Saga Furs, said: 'It is important for us to have fur on the catwalk. If it's on the catwalk, then it's in catalogues and people buy it. London is important not in terms of sales but in terms of talent. It's good to work with London designers, it's good for PR.'

Furriers insist that their product is ethically produced but this is disputed by designers who have visited the factories and by animal rights activists.

The headquarters of Saga Furs is a mansion in the Danish countryside. One designer who had been a guest of the company, said: 'It is not ethical at all. The animals are confined, they are in small, cramped spaces, they are not running around, they do not have a natural life. The furriers may say it's humane but it depends on what you call humane.'

People for the Ethical Treatment of Animals (PETA) says that confined animals suffer from intense boredom, many so severely that they display neurotic behaviours such as pacing and turning in endless circles.

'Most people in this country recognise that the fur industry is totally cruel and want nothing to do with it,' said the director of special projects at PETA. 'There is nothing fashionable about the ways animals die for their fur. The companies are always going to maximise their profits at the expense of their animals. It is a violent, bloody industry. There is no nice way to rip the fur off an animal's back.'

Audience needs and responses

My learning objectives ▶

This lesson will help you to:
- **look at text from the point of view of what an audience, or reader, needs**
- **consider ways readers might respond to texts.**

Audience needs

Remind yourself of what you learned in Chapter 2 about audience. You have seen how writers have an audience in mind when they produce documents to be read. This lesson reinforces that point. It also asks you to put yourself in the position of being the audience the text is written for.

This will help you to:

▶ understand what the writer's intention is in writing the text

▶ have a better understanding of what people want or need from a text

▶ suggest an appropriate response to the text.

You have also seen that a writer may have more than one audience in mind when a text is written.

Activity 1

Look again at the 'Careers for you' article on page 20.
We said that the audiences for 'Careers for you' are:
- people who are interested in catering
- people who want a goal or ambition to work towards.

Put yourself in the position of a person in each of these groups and write down briefly what you would *need* from a leaflet or website about working in the catering industry.

The audience of a text is often people who are reading for a purpose. They have a specific *need* and they will use leaflets, articles, the web and other documents as they search for information. Their sources of information will include pictures, and as you have seen in this chapter, the texts will often have lots of other things going on including presentation of different points of view, bias and persuasion.

Activity 2

Now try to identify different needs people might have when they seek out, find or obtain information from a text.

Remind yourself of:

- the 'Glastonbury Festival' information text, including the picture (page 33)
- the '20 highest revenue generating football clubs in the world' bar chart (page 35)
- the 'Fur companies lure designers' text (page 38).

Now jot down your response to the questions that follow.

1 How could the Glastonbury text satisfy the needs of:

   a somebody thinking of going to a festival

   b someone who wants to object to the festival taking place

   c someone who wants to work at the festival

   d someone thinking of camping at the festival?

2 How could the football club bar chart help the needs of:

   a a Manchester United fan

   b somebody writing an article about money in football

   c the writer of Arsenal's fanzine?

3 How could the fur companies text have relevance for the needs of:

   a British fashion designers

   b members of animal rights organisations

   c a catwalk model?

Suitable response

You have learned that there are many different sorts of text with different purposes. But someone who reads a document which gives information may or may not respond to it.

In the examples on pages 33, 35 and 38, the people who need information from the texts may or may not do anything when they get it. If a text is intended to be persuasive, however, there is a greater expectation that the audience or reader will respond.

You will be able to understand the meaning of a text better if you can work out what an appropriate response would be.

Activity 3

1   Look back at the leaflet 'Hundreds of children live on the streets' (page 22). You were studying this because it is effectively presented. Now think about what the writer of the leaflet really wants you to do once you've read it. Which of these do you think is the closest to what the writer wants?

   a   For you to find out some more information about Bogotá.

   b   For you to use the leaflet as a basis for a talk to your class.

   c   For you to try to organise some donations to help the YMCA.

   How would you go about responding appropriately to this leaflet?

2   Now look again at the 'Fur companies lure designers' text (page 38) and the three different audiences of: British fashion designers, members of animal rights organisations, and catwalk models.

   a   Write down one way that each of those audiences might respond to reading the text.

   b   What is your personal reaction to reading the text? How might you respond?

Peer/Self-assessment activity

In this chapter you have learned and practised some skills to do with being able to read and understand texts at Level 2. Before you do a short test, think about the work you have been doing and how confident you are about what you have learned. Then tick the boxes which are closest to how you feel.

Skill	Not confident	Need some more support	Very confident
I understand what *relevant information* means and can find it in a text, graph or picture.			
I understand what *point of view, implicit meaning* and *bias* mean and can detect them in a text.			
I can understand what different audiences need from texts and how they respond to them.			

Level 2 mini Reading test

Now use what you have learned to do the tests that follow. The focuses for these tests are to:

- select and use different types of text to obtain and utilise relevant information
- detect a point of view, implicit meaning and/or bias.

Read Test Source C and then complete the **two** tests. One asks you to write your answers down, the other is multiple-choice.

Test Source C

File   Edit   View   Favorites   Tools   Help

Address   http://www.vegsoc.org/parkdale/whatis2.html   Go   Links »

| Home | About Us | Latest | Support Us | Lifestyle | Food | Info | Veggie Approved | Young Veggie |

Vegetarian SOCIETY

Why do we need a Vegetarian Society?

Vegetarianism is growing and becoming more mainstream, but vegetarians are still only a small proportion of the population. The quality and range of vegetarian food has improved enormously over the years, but it's not enough. We have helped make life easier for millions of vegetarians, but we're not satisfied. Sweets, desserts and many prescription drugs still contain gelatine. Most wines and beers still don't say whether or not they were produced using animal products. Your relatives probably still think it's a phase you're going through and the dictionaries aren't sure whether or not vegetarians eat fish.

Common causes of food intolerance

The most common food intolerances, in order of frequency are milk, eggs, nuts, fish/shellfish, wheat/flour, chocolate, artificial colours, pork/bacon, chicken, tomato, soft fruit, cheese and yeast. Whilst not all food intolerances are related to meat and dairy products, it can be seen from the above list that vegetarians, and particularly vegans, will suffer less from food intolerance because they already eliminate some of the most common causes of intolerance.

Basic nutrition

Many people worry that when they stop eating meat and fish, they might be in danger of some nutritional deficiency. This is not the case as all the nutrients you need can easily be obtained from a vegetarian diet. In fact research shows that in many ways a vegetarian diet is the most beneficial.

Nutrients are usually divided into five classes: carbohydrates, proteins, fats (including oil), vitamins and minerals. We also need fibre and water. All are equally important to our well-being, although they are needed in varying quantities. Most foods contain a mixture of nutrients but it is convenient to classify them by the main nutrient they provide. Still, it is worth remembering that everything you eat gives you a whole range of essential nutrients.

Meat supplies protein, fat, some B vitamins and minerals (mostly iron, zinc, potassium and phosphorous). Fish, in addition to the above, supplies vitamins A, D, and E, and the mineral iodine.

All these nutrients can be easily obtained by vegetarians from other sources as our information sheets at http://www.vegsoc.org/ will show you.

Test 1

Read Test Source C opposite which is from the Vegetarian Society website and then answer the following questions. You need to write your answers in full sentences using your own words as far as possible.

1   Give three reasons why the writer thinks there should be a Vegetarian Society.
2   Name three foods which are a cause of food intolerance.
3   Write down three things you have learned from the text about nutrients.
4   What do you think the writer's view is of being a vegetarian or a vegan?
5   Do you think that this website has an implicit message for people?
    Explain your answer.

Test 2

Questions C1 to C5 refer to Test Source C. For each question select the right answer from A, B, C or D.

C1   The text tells you that:
  A   most wines and beers are suitable for vegetarians
  B   most young people today are vegetarian or vegan
  C   the range of food for vegetarians has improved
  D   you can find what 'vegan' means in a dictionary.

C2   The text informs you that:
  A   pork and bacon are good for you
  B   nuts commonly cause food intolerance
  C   most food intolerance is meat-related
  D   vegans are prone to food intolerances.

C3   From the text you learn that:
  A   eating meat will produce nutrient deficiencies
  B   fibre and water are important nutrients
  C   you get the mineral iodine from eating meat
  D   you can get your nutrients from a meat-free diet.

C4   The text implies that:
  A   vegetarians are healthier than meat-eaters
  B   it's better to be a vegetarian than to be a vegan
  C   you should encourage children to drink milk
  D   vegetarianism is becoming far too popular.

C5   The writer is of the view that:
  A   life is now easier for thousands of people
  B   more people should become vegetarian
  C   being vegetarian is a phase that passes
  D   food intolerance is a national disgrace.

TestZone

Student sample answers

Here are three student responses to Test 1 on the Vegetarian Society text (page 42). Read the answers together with the examiner comments beside and after the answers. First, remind yourself of the text and the questions (pages 42–43).

Student A Pass ✓

1 The writer wants a vegetarian society because most wines and beers don't say whether or not they were made using animal products. ✓ Sweets and many prescription drugs contain gelatine ✓ and because there are a growing amount of vegetarians. ✓

Full, clear and detailed response to the question.

2 Milk, ✓ eggs ✓ and nuts ✓ are the three main causes of food intolerance.

Full, clear and detailed response to the question.

3 From the text I have learned that nutrients are usually divided into five classes. ✓ In many ways a vegetarian diet is more beneficial ✓ and that meat contains protein, fat, B vitamins and minerals. ✓

Full, clear and detailed response to the question.

4 I think the writer thinks that vegetarians are more healthy and better off than if they ate meat. ✓

One point made of the three in the mark scheme.

5 I think the website is saying that it is better to be a vegetarian ✓ and eating meat is bad. ✓

The implicit meaning is understood, two points made which can score marks.

Examiner comment

The student has responded clearly and appropriately with the necessary detail in questions 1, 2 and 3 to gain full marks. The student gains only one point for question 4 where the mark scheme indicates a possible three points. For question 5 the student has understood the implicit meaning in the text and made two, albeit closely related, points. The score is 12/15 and would achieve Level 2.

Student B *Borderline* ✓✓✗

1 The writer thinks there should be a vegetarian society because only a small proportion of the population are vegetarians. ✓ Another reason why is because the quality and range of vegetarian food has improved but it's not enough ✓ but at the same time gelatine contains some drugs. ✓

> Three points made, two of them clearly; understanding shown.

2 Three foods which are a cause of food intolerance are milk, ✓ eggs ✓ and nuts. ✓

> Full, clear and detailed response to the question.

3 Three things I have learned from the text about nutrition are that many people worry that when they stop eating meat and fish they might be in danger of some nutritional deficiency. ✓ Another thing I've learned is nutrients are usually divided into five classes. ✓ Finally everything we eat gives you a whole range of essential nutrients. ✓

> Full, clear and detailed response to the question.

4 I think the writer's view about being a vegetarian or vegan is fair because they say about what you need and what nutrients you get eating and not eating meat. ✗

> This is not a valid response to the question; the question is about the writer's view of vegetarianism, not the student's view of the writer.

5 I think the website does have an implicit message for people because it shows two points of view. ✗

> The response makes an undeveloped point which does not address the question.

Examiner comment

The student scored full marks on the first three questions which asked for facts or information to be retrieved from the text. However, the two questions which required interpretation or judgement were not successful. The student would need to practise working out exactly what the questions are asking, particularly questions focused on overall, general interpretations of the text. A score of 9/15 would probably be enough for Level 2, but the overall performance is borderline.

TestZone

Student C Fail ✗

1 There is more food for the vegetarians. ✗

> This is a limited – and incorrect – answer. The point in the text is that the range has improved, not just that there's more.

2 The names of the foods which cause intolerance are:
   milk, ✓ eggs ✓ and nuts. ✓

> Full, clear and detailed response to the question.

3 The three things that I have learned from the text about nutrients are:
   a If you stop eating meat and fish it will not affect the nutrients going into your body. ✓
   b Research says that in many ways a vegetarian diet is easier to get nutrients. ✓
   c Nutrients are usually divided into five classes: carbohydrates, proteins, fats, vitamins and minerals. ✓

> Full, clear and detailed response to the question.

4 I think the writer's view about being a vegetarian or a vegan is that he likes it because vegetarian foods have improved. ✓

> The mark has been given on a 'benefit of the doubt' basis since 'he likes it' implies a positive view of vegetarianism.

5 Yes, because it tells you that being a vegetarian isn't all that bad for you. ✗

> This is not a valid response to the question. The response does not indicate anything implicit.

Examiner comment

The student did not complete question 1, possibly by not reading the question carefully, and had difficulty with the questions which needed interpretation and judgement. The student's response to question 3 was very good. However, a mark of 7/15 would not achieve Level 2.

Peer/Self-assessment activity

1 Compare the answers you and your partner wrote with the answers from Student A. Can you find another five reasons in response to question 1?

2 Questions 4 and 5 refer to 'implicit' meanings in a text; Student A does this well. Compare your response to Student A's answer.

3 Look at Student B's response to question 4. How has the student misunderstood the question?

4 Discuss with your partner why you think Student C received no marks for questions 1 and 5?

5 Why is Student C's answer to question 5 not 'implicit'? Discuss what 'implicit' means with your partner (see page 36 for further detail).

6 What was your response to question 4?

7 Write down three or four ways you now feel more confident about answering questions on texts like these.

In the future…
You have been studying a variety of examples of texts. Choose one of the texts and write some of your own questions to make a test. Swap with your partner and see how you both get on.

Skill standard

Make a range of contributions to discussions in a range of contexts, including those that are unfamiliar, and make effective presentations.

What you need to do:

▶ Consider complex information and give a relevant, cogent response in appropriate language.

▶ Present information and ideas clearly and persuasively to others.

▶ Adapt contributions to suit audience, purpose and situation.

▶ Make significant contributions to discussions, taking a range of roles and helping to move discussion forward.

Your teacher or tutor will help you to decide whether to use the following tasks. They will also help you to organise the tasks should you attempt them.

Task 1: Presentation

This is a research-based topic for four students. Read the article 'Fur companies lure designers' (page 38). The issue of killing animals for their fur has been debated for many years.

Do some research on this topic using Internet and library sources. You might also find some clothing retailers who sell real fur items and get their point of view.

One pair should present an argument in favour of controlled use of real fur for retail. The other pair should present an argument opposing them. Make the presentation as a forum to the class but keep your contributions individual.

Task 2: Discussion

In a group of four, discuss whether a music festival should be allowed in your area. You might include the following in your discussion:

▶ The benefits to your area, such as:
  - enjoying the music
  - raising awareness of your area
  - bringing money to your area.

▶ Any negative impacts, such as:
  - noise pollution
  - road congestion
  - anti-social behaviour.

You could decide to take different points of view in your discussion. Two of you could be in favour of the idea and two of you against.

My learning ▶

This lesson will help you to:
- understand the content of a newspaper article, including headline and pictures
- obtain relevant information from a text.

Obtaining relevant information from a text

Introduction

Between them, Chapters 2 and 3 cover the Level 2 skill standards listed on page vii. These chapters include a variety of texts that:

▶ give information and explanation ('Careers for you', page 20)

▶ describe and persuade ('Hundreds of children die on the streets', page 22)

▶ offer information with a point of view or bias ('Glastonbury Festival', page 33)

▶ present ideas and arguments for and against ('Fur companies lure designers', page 38)

This chapter puts together all the skills covered in Chapters 2 and 3.

Key words and phrases

First read the article on page 49, which is from the *Daily Mail* online edition. Then complete Activity 1 below.

Activity 1

1 There are six paragraphs in the article. Copy and complete the table below by filling in the key words and phrases from each paragraph. The first paragraph has been done for you.

Paragraph	Key words and phrases
1	local postman, bike, staple of British life, change, egg-shaped vehicle, trialled, mass order
2	
3	
4	
5	
6	

Now test yourself and a partner by answering the following questions. You can do this orally.

2 What is the 'change' the article is writing about?

3 Where is the trial taking place?

4 Describe the vans which the Royal Mail use now.

5 How is the Matra environmentally friendly?

6 What might the Matra replace?

7 What are the benefits of the Matra?

If you can answer all of the questions you will have *obtained relevant information* from the article.

http://www.dailymail.co.uk/news/article-1168292/French-egg-shaped-buggy-spell-end-humble-British-postman-bike.html

Home | News | Sport | TV&Showbiz | Femail | Health | Science&Tech | Money | Debate | Coffee Break | Property | Motoring | Travel

News Home | World news | Headlines | Pictures | Most read | News Board

French egg-shaped buggy could spell the end of the humble British postman on his bike

By *Daily Mail* Reporter

The local postman delivering letters on his bike has been a staple of British life for years – but it could be all change thanks to the French. An egg-shaped vehicle – with a top speed of just 25mph – is being trialled in two areas and could lead to a mass order by Royal Mail.

In a move which could upset traditionalists but please saddle-sore postmen, the odd-looking buggies could put an end to the use of bicycles within the postal service.

Royal Mail fleet manager Craig Lightfoot said that if the three-month trial in Oxford proved a success, the Matra model, which is also used on the Continent, could replace a fleet of diesel Vauxhall Combo vans.

'We're looking at ways of becoming more environmentally friendly and these vehicles are well-suited to town deliveries. Some cycles could be phased out if postmen start sharing these vehicles in future. We have about 19 Vauxhall vans in our fleet here, so ultimately the Matra could replace them.'

The Matra has a range of 30 to 35 miles once its battery has been fully charged. The vehicle is officially classed as a quadracycle, and like a motorbike is not legally required to display a front number plate.

Mr Lightfoot estimated that the Matra would be about 35 per cent cheaper than a traditional diesel-engined van. He added that the electric vehicle cost the equivalent of a new hatchback car, compared with the £10,000 cost of the Vauxhall Combo.

The Matra, built in France

Children's favourite: Postman Pat and his faithful black and white cat Jess

My learning objectives ▶

This lesson will help you to:
- read and summarise, succinctly, information/ideas from different sources
- identify the purposes of texts
- understand how meaning is conveyed.

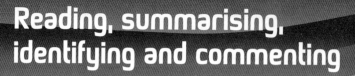

Reading, summarising, identifying and commenting

Summarising a text

There are pieces of information in the article on page 49 and there are other ideas. In the first paragraph there are two pieces of information.

1 The local postman (or woman) delivers letters on a bike.

2 An egg-shaped vehicle is being tried out.

There is also the idea that the local postman delivering letters on his bike has been a part of British life for years, and the idea that the change is thanks to the French.

Activity 1

1 Using the key words and phrases table you completed in Activity 1 on page 48, rewrite the article in six sentences.

2 Now reduce your six sentences to two:
- one will be about what is going on, generally, with the trial
- the other will contain the main details of the Matra.

3 Finally, write a single sentence which combines all the information from the two sentences.

Key term

Here's a reminder of what you do when you make a **summary**:
- **give the main points**
- **give a run-down**
- **outline**
- **review**
- **sum up**
- **make a synopsis**
- **put in a nutshell.**

Identify the purposes of texts

Here are some purposes for writing which you have met before, plus a few new ones:

report	instruct	explain	advise
argue	describe	analyse	review
inform	complain	comment	express a point of view.

Activity 2

1 Re-read the article and your summary of it from Activity 1 above. Write down what you think the writer is trying to achieve in the article.

2 Now decide the main purpose in writing the article. Select the most appropriate word from the purposes list above.

3 Discuss with a partner whether or not the writer might have had other purposes in writing the piece. Choose some words from the list above for these.

How meaning is conveyed

When you are asked to consider how meaning is conveyed, remember you need to think about:

▶ the layout – how the paragraphs, headline and pictures combine

▶ the effectiveness of the headline

▶ the writer's choice of certain words and phrases

▶ the pictures and captions – what effect they have on the reader.

Activity 3

You are going to concentrate on the pictures in the *Daily Mail* article on page 49. Discuss with a partner and write down your responses to the questions below.

The Matra, built in France

Childrens favourite: Postman Pat and his faithful black and white cat Jess

1   What do the pictures show?
2   How are they serious or humorous?
3   Are they cleverly combined? If so, in what way and to what effect?
4   How do they relate to the text?
5   Do they help your understanding? If so, how?
6   Do they give the text added meaning? If so, how?

This lesson will help you to:
- detect a point of view, implicit meaning and/or bias
- analyse texts in relation to audience needs and consider suitable responses.

Detecting implicit meaning and analysing texts

Detect a point of view, implicit meaning and/or bias

You know what the article on page 49 is about, what information it is giving you. But is there something more going on? Is the writer trying to put across a particular point of view? Is the author biased in any way? Is there an implicit or hidden meaning to the article?

Remember what you learned about these words:

▶ *implicit meaning* means something other than the main meaning of the text, something implied, suggested, hidden, beneath the surface

▶ *bias* means partial to, prejudiced about, in favour of, inclined towards or against.

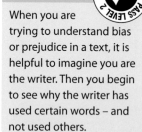

When you are trying to understand bias or prejudice in a text, it is helpful to imagine you are the writer. Then you begin to see why the writer has used certain words – and not used others.

Activity 1

1 Re-read the article, but this time from the point of view of someone who is not in favour of changing to the Matra.

2 Write down the words and phrases which might imply a bias against the introduction of the Matra for example, 'odd-looking buggies'.

3 Is there anything in the headline which suggests an implicit meaning?

> ### French egg-shaped buggy could spell the end of the humble British postman on his bike

4 Does the Postman Pat picture add anything to the idea of implicit meaning or bias?

5 If you think there is evidence that the journalist has a biased view, write that view down in one or two sentences.

In a multiple-choice test you will sometimes find you can't make your mind up which is the right answer. You need to look carefully at the wording of the question and think carefully about the audience and purpose of the text. Remember there is only ONE right answer.

Analyse texts in relation to audience needs and consider suitable responses

In your Level 2 Reading test you need to consider suitable responses to the texts you read. For example, people who read the article on the *Daily Mail* website were invited by the website to send in their comments by email. Here are a few of those comments:

▶ 'We need to be environmentally friendly … stay on your bike!'

▶ 'How long does the battery last in winter with lights, heater and wipers on?'

▶ 'So why is the Royal Mail trialling a French 25mph traffic-blocker?'

Activity 2

Write the draft of an email to send to the *Daily Mail* with your comment on the article.

Peer/Self-assessment activity

This chapter repeats the skills for Level 2, bringing them all together. Here they are listed again so that you can ask yourself how well you have understood the Reading chapters of the book. Tick the boxes closest to how you feel.

Skill	Not confident	Need some more support	Very confident
Select and use different types of text to obtain and utilise relevant information.			
Read and summarise, succinctly, information/ideas from different sources.			
Identify the purposes of texts and comment on how meaning is conveyed.			
Detect point of view, implicit meaning and/or bias.			
Analyse texts in relation to audience needs and consider suitable responses.			

TestZone

Level 2 mini Reading test

Now use what you have learned to do the tests that follow. This Reading test covers **all** of the Level 2 skill standards.

Read Test Source D and then complete the **two** tests. One asks you to write your answers down, the other is multiple-choice.

Test Source D

http://www.dofe.org/What_is_a_DofE_prog.aspx

What is a DofE programme?

A DofE programme is a real adventure from beginning to end. It doesn't matter who you are or where you're from. You just need to be aged between 14 and 24 and realise there's more to life than sitting on a sofa watching life pass you by.

You can do programmes at three levels, Bronze, Silver or Gold, which lead to a Duke of Edinburgh's Award.

You'll find yourself helping people or the community, getting fitter, developing skills, going on an expedition and taking part in a residential activity.

But here's the best bit – you get to choose what you do!

Why should I do it?

Good question!

Because, from the first day to the last it's a real adventure. Every section gives you something different – that's the fun of it!

You'll enjoy loads of new experiences, discover talents you never thought you had, challenge yourself and meet lots of people just like you. Also, you'll do things you love and get a kick out of. It's a real buzz!

Then there's all the other stuff ...

... achieving an Award will give you skills, confidence and a view on life that everyone is looking for, from employers to colleges and universities.

... you'll be recognised for doing things you've chosen to do.

... and you'll make a difference to other people's lives and your community, be fitter and healthier, make new friends and have memories to last you a lifetime.

The question should really be why wouldn't you bother!

How do I get the Award?

You achieve an Award by completing a personal programme of activities in four sections (five if you're going for Gold).

These sections are:
- Volunteering – helping someone, your community or the environment
- Physical – becoming fitter through sport, dance or fitness activities
- Skills – developing existing talents or trying something new
- Expedition – planning, training for and completing an adventurous journey
- Residential (Gold only) – staying and working away from home as part of a team.

The length of time you have to spend on each section depends on the level of programme you're doing.

For more information go to the Home page.

Test 1

Read Test Source D carefully which is taken from the Duke of Edinburgh's Award website, then answer the following questions. You need to write your answers in full sentences using your own words as far as possible.

1   What information about the D of E programme do you learn from the text?

2   In what ways does the writer of the text try to persuade you that doing a D of E programme is a good idea?

3   How many different levels of programme are there?

4   Explain how doing a D of E programme might help you in real life.

5   What is involved in the 'Volunteering' and the 'Expedition' sections?

6   Explain what you think the writer's view is of people who just hang around 'sitting on a sofa'.

7   Do you think the layout of the writing is effective? If so, explain why.

8   What are the top two pictures showing? How do they relate to the writing?

Test 2

Questions D1 to D5 refer to Test Source D. For each question select the right answer from A, B, C or D.

D1   The main purpose of the text is to:

    A   persuade people to sponsor a D of E programme

    B   give you information about the D of E Award scheme

    C   persuade you to enroll in a D of E programme today

    D   encourage you to go camping at weekends.

D2   The text tells you that:

    A   within the programme you choose what you do

    B   there are four levels of programme available

    C   there is no age limit to doing the D of E Award

    D   everybody has to complete the Residential section.

D3   The text gets its meaning across effectively because:

    A   it uses lots of emotive language

    B   it shows pictures of people on their holidays

    C   it quotes the opinion of experts

    D   it uses paragraphs and bullet points clearly.

D4   The text implies that:

    A   doing a D of E programme is not worth the bother

    B   the Award is unlikely to benefit you in getting a job

    C   being a couch potato is a rather pathetic way of life

    D   it's only really worth going for the Gold Level Award.

D5   From what you have read, which of the following would be the most suitable action?

    A   Send your local D of E centre some photos of you camping.

    B   Organise sponsorship events to raise money for local D of E groups.

    C   Look at the D of E homepage to find out more about the programme.

    D   Write to your MP complaining about the lack of community volunteers.

Student sample answers

Here are three student responses to Test 1 on the Duke of Edinburgh's Award text (page 54). Read the answers together with the examiner comments around and after the answers. First, remind yourself of the text and the questions (pages 54–55).

Student A *Pass* ✓

1 The information you gain from Duke of Edinburgh is that anyone can join if you are between 14–24, ✓ that you help in the community ✓ and develop lots of new skills. ✓

> Three clear and appropriate points are made from a possible eight identified in the mark scheme. Each tick is a half mark.

2 The writer persuades you that it will be a good idea by telling you that you will have fun ✓ and gain an award from it. ✓

> Two clear points are made from a possible eight identified on the mark scheme; 'an award' is valid. Each tick is a half mark.

3 There are three different levels, Bronze, Silver and Gold. ✓

> The correct answer is given.

4 Doing the Duke of Edinburgh you will become fitter, ✓ find out new skills ✓ and you will gain confidence. ✓ It will help with jobs as it is impressive to employers. ✓

> Clear and full response given. 'Fitter' is ticked but the maximum mark is three.

5 In volunteering you will help others in the community and help the local environment. ✓ Expeditions involve planning and training for adventures. ✓

> The two sections are correctly and clearly described by the student.

6 They believe that people who sit and watch TV all the time are wasting their lives. ✓ There are so many other things you could be doing. ✓

> The student makes two clear and appropriate points.

7 I think the layout is effective as the sub headings make it easier to understand. ✓ The pictures persuade you as they are all having fun. ✓ There is little colour as it's aimed at 14 year olds and up. ✓

> Two points made which show a clear understanding of layout with explanations offered. The third point is given as a valid interpretation.

8 The pictures show camping and a group of friends. The camping links with the expedition side. ✓ The second picture shows that you will make friends through it. ✓

> Both parts of the question are addressed succinctly but clearly.

Examiner comment

The student has shown a full and clear understanding of the text. Marks were lost on the first two questions because of lack of detail. If a question does not specify a number of points to be made, then as many as possible should be included. The student was strong on the interpretation of the text. The mark is 15½/21 which would achieve Level 2.

Student B *Borderline* ✓✓✗

1 From the text you learn what the D of E is, for instance it gives you information on what the objective of the D of E is and the contents of what's in store for people who join or get involved in the D of E. ✗

> The answer is general, vague and not specific, there are no scoring points made.

2 The writer of the D of E website tries to persuade the reader to join D of E by saying that when doing it you can get fitter, ✓ develop more skills, ✓ and take part in things to do with your community to help others ✓ and also yourself. ✓

> Four points clearly made out of eight in the mark scheme.

3 There are three different levels of the programme, Bronze, Silver and Gold ✓. With all three there are four activities you can do, but with gold there are five you have to do to achieve an Award.

> There is one mark for the '3 levels'; the rest of the answer is not asked for and does not score.

4 By doing a D of E Award you can achieve many new skills ✓ and techniques: this can help you get a higher level in a job than you would do if you didn't have the skills.

> The student has really only made one point; the point made in the text about employers and colleges is not made here.

5 In Volunteering you can help the environment, your local community and the people in that community. ✓ But Expedition is more adventurous, such as planning, training for and completing an adventurous journey. ✓

> A full and clear answer to the question.

6 The writer's view of people who just spend their time sitting on a sofa watching life pass by is that they are lazy ✓ and are wasting their life and time when they could be doing something else. ✓

> There are two points here closely related to the mark scheme.

7 I think the writing is really well done. It has parts ✓ where it makes you look back on another part to continue on the part you are on already.

> The point about structure is just about made followed by a rather muddled idea.

8 The pictures are pictures of people doing the activities with friends and enjoying their time doing it. ✓

> The answer is rather general but makes the point about enjoyment.

Examiner comment

The student's comments are general in places and not focused on the question asked. The response to question 1 lacks anything specific. However, a good basic understanding of the text is shown. The mark of 10/21 would be a borderline score at Level 2

Student C *Fail* X

Two clear points made out of eight in the mark scheme (half mark each).

1   The information you get is that you can be between 14–24 ✓ and it is a real adventure. ✓

Two clear points; 'getting awards' is not in the text and is confused with what 'achieving an Award will give you...'. Each tick is a half mark.

2   They try persuading you by saying that you learn new skills, ✓ you get awards and that it helps the community. ✓

3   There are 3 levels, Gold, Silver and Bronze. ✓

The answer is correct and clearly stated.

4   It may help you in future life, as it gives you skills ✓ and team building for the future.

One clear point; there is no mention in the text of 'team building'.

5   In the volunteering section you are involved with helping someone and the community or environment. ✓ In the expedition section you are involved with planning, training for and completing an adventurous journey. ✓

Clear and correct response.

6   The writer's view of sitting on the sofa and watching television is that they are lazy ✓ and missing life. ✓

Two points are made though the second needs development.

7   The layout is OK, it is not that interesting and I would not read it, this is because it is all the same with hardly any colour, making it boring to read. ✓

There is a comment about lack of colour but the student has missed all of the structural aspects of the text.

8   The pictures show people having fun on the trip. The writing does not relate to me. Though the pictures do, as they make it look fun. ✓

The idea of fun is mentioned but the comments on the pictures are very limited. Half a mark would be given.

Examiner comment

The student missed marks on the first two questions because of a lack of detail. In the last two questions, the responses were limited and contained somewhat inappropriate comments. The total mark of 9½/21 would not achieve Level 2.

Peer/Self-assessment activity

1   Compare the answers you and your partner wrote with the answers from Student A. Questions 1, 2 and 4 are 'retrieval' questions where the student has taken information from the text. How are you answers different?

2   How many more things about layout can you now find in answer to question 7?

3   Student A achieved Level 2. What did Student A do that you didn't?

4   Look at Student C's answer to questions 7 and 8. Discuss what is wrong with them.

5   Questions 6, 7 and 8 need 'interpretation' not just 'retrieval' from the text. Student C fails to do this for question 7. How well does Student B do?

6   Discuss how well you and your partner responded to the 'interpretation' questions.

In the future…

▶   Look at some of the texts you have brought in, remembering what you have learned about 'interpreting' questions.

▶   Make some 'interpretation' comments about the layout and pictures used in the texts.

Skill standard

Make a range of contributions to discussions in a range of contexts, including those that are unfamiliar, and make effective presentations.

What you need to do:

▶ Consider complex information and give a relevant, cogent response in appropriate language.

▶ Present information and ideas clearly and persuasively to others.

▶ Adapt contributions to suit audience, purpose and situation.

▶ Make significant contributions to discussions, taking a range of roles and helping to move discussion forward.

Your teacher or tutor will help you to decide whether to use the following tasks. They will also help you to organise the tasks should you attempt them.

Task 1: Presentation

This is a research-based task asking what people do with their spare time.

The research might be conducted within your class, or peer group outside of school or college, to find out what people do to occupy their leisure time.

Your task is to find out how many people do anything 'worthwhile' in their leisure time such as keeping fit, voluntary work or work with organisations such as the Duke of Edinburgh's Award. Create a survey, with appropriate questions, to help you find out this information. Then carry the survey out on friends and classmates.

From the results of your survey, create and deliver a presentation. This could be purely informative or could present the information together with advice and persuasion.

Task 2: Discussion

In groups of four, discuss what you think is the best kind of holiday. For example, holidays can be very active (swimming, mountain climbing, wind-surfing and so on) or they can be very passive (sitting on the beach, reading books and so on).

You could try to take sides on this topic. Two of you could be in favour of active holidays and two in favour of more passive ones.

Section B
Writing

Functional Skills English: Writing

In the following chapters you will learn about the requirements for achieving Level 1 and Level 2 Functional Skills English in Writing. This is separate to Reading and you need to achieve your Level in each part (Reading, Writing, and Speaking, Listening and Communication) in order to gain your certificate.

The table on page 61 will take you through the skill standards for Level 1 and 2 Writing.

In Chapter 5 you will learn about:

▶ texts and documents
▶ using language, format and structure suitable for purpose and audience
▶ writing clearly, coherently and in appropriate detail
▶ presenting information in a logical sequence
▶ grammar, spelling and punctuation.

The Functional Skills English skill standard for Level 2 Writing is really in two parts: content and accuracy. The 'content' is what you write and the 'accuracy' is how you write it. For Level 2 there are three content elements and three accuracy elements, including one about sentence structures.

The Level 2 skill standard requires you to be able to write informatively and to write persuasively.

Chapter 6 will cover:

▶ documents
▶ writing to inform clearly, concisely and logically
▶ writing to inform on complex subjects.

Chapter 7 will cover:

▶ writing to persuade
▶ using a range of different writing styles
▶ complex sentences and grammar points.

Peer/Self-assessment

Before starting each lesson, carefully read the skill standards opposite and the relevant 'My learning' section in each lesson – you will be given the opportunity to assess how well you have done on these before and after the Writing tests. You will also have the chance to compare your test answers with some sample student work.

Functional Skills English: Speaking, Listening and Communication

In each of the following chapters you will find suggested Speaking, Listening and Communication tasks. Your teacher or tutor will decide whether you will use these tasks and, if so, will also help adapt them to your needs.

Skill standards

Below are the skill standards for Levels 1 and 2, mapped to their coverage in this book.

Skill standard (Level 1)	Coverage and range	Coverage in the Student Book
Write a range of texts to communicate information, ideas and opinions using formats and styles suitable for their purpose and audience.	• Write clearly and coherently including an appropriate level of detail. • Present information in a logical sequence. • Use language, format and structure suitable for purpose and audience. • Use correct grammar, including correct and consistent use of tense. • Ensure written work includes accurate punctuation and spelling and that meaning is clear. In more than one type of text.	Pages 62–72

Skill standard (Level 2)	Coverage and range	Coverage in the Student Book
Write a range of texts, including extended written documents, communicating information, ideas and opinions, effectively and persuasively.	• Present information/ideas concisely, logically and persuasively.	Pages 78–89, 90–104
	• Present information on complex subjects clearly and concisely.	Pages 78–89, 90–104
	• Use a range of writing styles for different purposes.	Pages 78–89, 90–104
	• Use a range of writing sentence structures, including complex sentences, and paragraphs to organise written communication effectively.	Pages 78–89, 90–104
	• Punctuate written text using commas, apostrophes and inverted commas accurately.	Pages 78–89, 90–104
	• Ensure written work is fit for purpose and audience, with accurate spelling and grammar that support clear meaning. In a range of text types.	Pages 78–89, 90–104

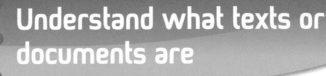

My learning ▶

This lesson will help you to:
- understand what texts or documents are
- understand the various purposes for documents.

Understand what texts or documents are

Types of texts and their purposes

In your test you will be asked to write one or more texts, perhaps as many as three. There are lots of texts, or documents, you come across in everyday life, such as:

books	pamphlets	application forms
emails	text messages	business and personal letters
licences	leaflets	greetings cards
notices	notes	articles in magazines and newspapers

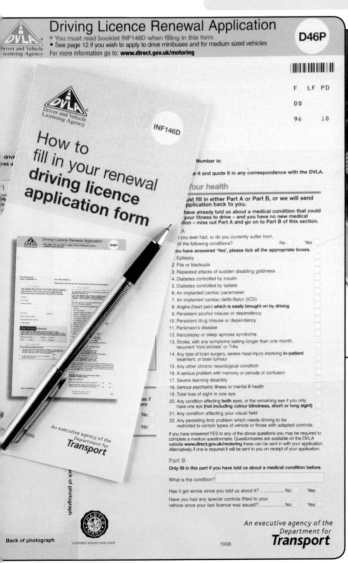

In your test you will be writing documents to communicate with others. Their purpose will be to convey something, such as information, ideas, opinions, requests and so on.

You will need to be clear what sorts of document you are being asked to write and for what purpose. The writing tasks you are set will tell you this. Each writing question will give you guidance about the type of document required and its purpose. You should read the writing questions carefully.

Activity 1

1   Match the writing purpose to the document type. The first one has been done for you. The others are mixed up.

Purpose		Document type
1 Writing to complain about poor service		**A** Business letter of complaint
2 Writing about a football match for the school magazine		**B** Handout
3 Writing to try to get a job		**C** Advertisement
4 Writing about how to change an ink cartridge		**D** Article
5 Writing your views on new school buildings for the school magazine		**E** Information leaflet
6 Writing to tell people about a new bus service		**F** Magazine review
7 Writing about a forthcoming event – to be given out to people		**G** Instruction sheet
8 Writing to get people to buy a new product		**H** Letter of application
9 Writing to apply for a passport		**I** Report
10 Writing about a film you have seen		**J** Application form

2   Work with a partner to make a list of documents you have come across in the last few days. The types of document mentioned so far in this lesson will help you. Use a table like this one.

The document	Where you came across it	Its purpose

My learning objectives ▶

This lesson will help you to:
- understand what writing clearly and coherently means
- understand what writing in an appropriate level of detail means.

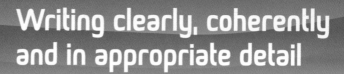

Writing clearly, coherently and in appropriate detail

The skill standard (which is listed on page 61) is really in two parts – content and accuracy. The first three bullets are 'content' and the last two are 'accuracy'. The content is what you write and the accuracy is how you write it; accuracy is also about how you use sentences.

The examiner will be awarding you marks according to how **clearly** and **coherently** you put down your ideas.

You also need to write in the appropriate level of detail. This means that you should only include the ideas or information you have been asked for and nothing else.

The text below is an example of writing that is clear, coherent and appropriate, as the annotated version on page 65 shows you. First, read the text, then complete Activity 1 which follows on the next page.

Key terms

Clearly means:
- straightforward
- well organised
- definite
- un-cluttered
- uncomplicated
- simple

Coherently means:
- easy to understand
- easy to follow
- orderly
- hanging together well

To Head Teachers

This leaflet is designed to reduce the number of fire-related accidents in schools.

Young children must rely on you to handle any school fire emergency, and, as the Head of the school, it is your responsibility to do everything in your power to reduce, control and eliminate conditions that may lead to a fire.

Always take school fire drills seriously and evacuate the school when the alarm sounds. You must also inform the fire brigade when an alarm has been raised.

You must hold fire drills on a regular basis. Have the initial fire drill for the school year in early September.

Ensure that school employees know how to evacuate their work areas and perform their fire drill duties in an emergency.

Always sound the alarm at the first sign of smoke or fire and be familiar with the location of the nearest fire alarm and extinguisher.

Learn how to operate fire extinguishers, fire blankets and fire hoses. Your fire department is available to provide instructions and demonstrations.

Activity 1

To test how effective this piece of writing is, answer the questions that follow. Refer to the annotated version of the text below to help you.

1　Who is the audience?
2　What is the purpose of the writing?
　　Hint: look at the first paragraph
3　What is the head teacher responsible for? Hint: look at the second paragraph.
4　Write down any four things the head teacher has to do.
5　How does the leaflet keep its focus through each of the paragraphs?
6　How many separate things are detailed for the head teacher to do?
7　With a partner, discuss how clear and coherent you think the leaflet is. Do you think that the school will be safer from fire if the writer's ideas are followed by the head teacher? Why?

To Head Teachers

This leaflet is designed to reduce the number of fire-related accidents in schools.

Young children must rely on you to handle any school fire emergency, and, as the Head of the school, it is your responsibility to do everything in your power to reduce, control and eliminate conditions that may lead to a fire.

Always take school fire drills seriously and evacuate the school when the alarm sounds. You must also inform the fire brigade when an alarm has been raised.

You must hold fire drills on a regular basis. Have the initial fire drill for the school year in early September.

Ensure that school employees know how to evacuate their work areas and perform their fire drill duties in an emergency.

Always sound the alarm at the first sign of smoke or fire and be familiar with the location of the nearest fire alarm and extinguisher.

Learn how to operate fire extinguishers, fire blankets and fire hoses. Your fire department is available to provide instructions and demonstrations.

Annotations:
- Clearly states the audience/reader
- Clearly states the purpose of the leaflet
- Clearly states the responsibility of the head teacher
- Re-states the purpose
- Clear, coherent and well ordered detail of what has to be done
- Concluding point

This lesson will help you to:
- understand what presenting information in a logical sequence means
- understand what scaffolding and planning your writing mean.

Presenting information in a logical sequence

It is important to present your ideas and information in a logical sequence. An example of a logical sequence might be that to pass your driving test you have to learn the manoeuvre sequence: Mirror, Signal, Manoeuvre – in that order.

Key term

Logical sequence means:
- clear
- organised
- put in order
- making sense
- not muddled up
- arranged properly
- one after the other
- first to last.

Some games and puzzles are based on sequences. For example, what are the two letters that follow the following sequence of letters?

M   T   W   T   F   ?   ?

Activity 1

Here's a sequencing challenge for you to solve. Read the list of a student's lessons below, then draw the student's timetable.

- Sarah has six lessons beginning with maths.
- Break comes in the middle of the morning's four lessons.
- ICT is in the afternoon.
- PE is directly after break.
- History is just before lunch.
- English is lesson two.
- She has music after ICT.
- Sarah ends the day with Homework Club.

For some functional writing the order is very important. A set of instructions for putting together a piece of furniture needs to be carefully written from the first part of the assembly to the last. The instructions would be useless otherwise.

Scaffolding and planning your writing

Other types of document also need careful sequencing. Sometimes the writing question will provide help. This is called scaffolding. Scaffolding gives you something to build on; it helps sequence your thoughts. If you follow the scaffolding in the question then your writing will hold together and make sense.

A writing plan follows the outline of your scaffolding but you will include more detail of what you will write in each section or paragraph of your writing. Here is an example of a writing question with some scaffolding:

> Safety in schools and colleges is important. Write a leaflet to be given to all students which informs them how to behave safely.
>
> Inform them about:
>
> - how they should move around the buildings
> - how to enter and leave classrooms
> - suitable clothing and footwear
> - proper behaviour in Science labs
> - how to behave if an alarm goes off.
>
> } Scaffolding

PASS LEVEL 1 Always follow the scaffolding which comes with the writing question in the test and always write a plan.

PASS LEVEL 1 Always write your answer plan in the answer book just before you start your neat writing. Draw a line under it but don't scribble it out. This way the examiner can see what your ideas were.

Activity 2

Using the question and scaffolding above, write a plan for your leaflet. You should jot down ideas for each of the bullet points above. For your plan, you could use a spider diagram like this:

Or you might prefer to use a writing frame like this:

Paragraph	Ideas/information content
1 Buildings	
2 Classrooms	
3 Clothing	
4 Science labs	
5 Fire alarm	

My learning objectives

This lesson will help you to:
- understand how to use language, format and structure.

Language, format and structure

Using language, format and structure

For some forms of writing you need to set out your writing in a particular way. One special time you will need to do this is when you are writing a letter of application for a job. Here is an example which explains the language, format and structure needed.

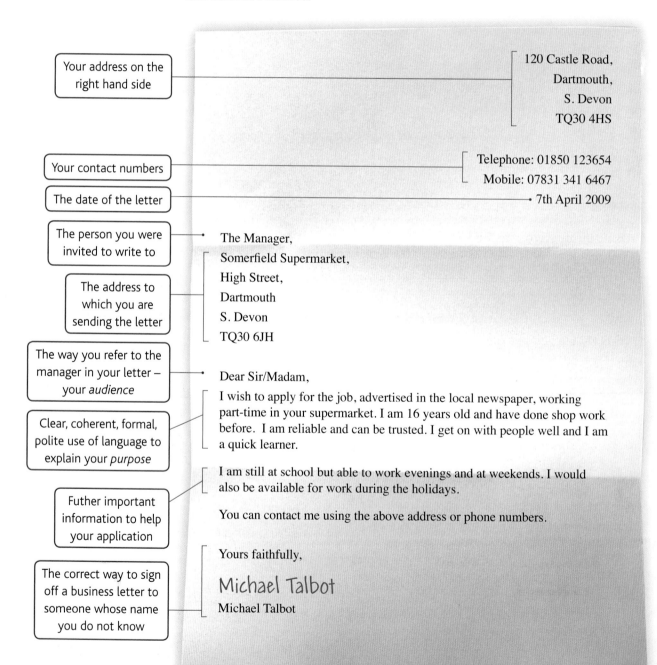

Your address on the right hand side

120 Castle Road,
Dartmouth,
S. Devon
TQ30 4HS

Your contact numbers

Telephone: 01850 123654
Mobile: 07831 341 6467

The date of the letter

7th April 2009

The person you were invited to write to

The Manager,
Somerfield Supermarket,

The address to which you are sending the letter

High Street,
Dartmouth
S. Devon
TQ30 6JH

The way you refer to the manager in your letter – your *audience*

Dear Sir/Madam,

Clear, coherent, formal, polite use of language to explain your *purpose*

I wish to apply for the job, advertised in the local newspaper, working part-time in your supermarket. I am 16 years old and have done shop work before. I am reliable and can be trusted. I get on with people well and I am a quick learner.

Futher important information to help your application

I am still at school but able to work evenings and at weekends. I would also be available for work during the holidays.

You can contact me using the above address or phone numbers.

Yours faithfully,

The correct way to sign off a business letter to someone whose name you do not know

Michael Talbot

Michael Talbot

A business letter needs to be formally structured, with language appropriate for the person it's being sent to and its purpose. There are a number of variations of this – for instance, if you do know the name of the person you are writing to you end the letter 'Yours sincerely'. But for your test, if you follow the format on the previous page, you'll get the marks!

You might have to make up some information to fit the task you are given, such as names and addresses. These need to be appropriate and sensible. You can practise doing so in the following activity.

Activity 1

1   Read the following question and the scaffolding that follows.
    Then write a full plan which includes the things you need to make up.

    You have seen an advertisement for a job in a shop window or local newspaper. Write a letter to the manager applying for the job.

    Tell the manager about:
    - *why you want the job*
    - *how you are suited to the job*
    - *any working experience you have*
    - *the times you can work*
    - *your availability to be interviewed.*

    For this activity you need to:
    - decide to use your own address or make one up
    - make up a sensible address for the shop
    - make up the name of the newspaper where you saw the job advertised
    - brainstorm some ideas for the scaffolding given in the question.

2   Now write your letter.

My learning objectives ▶

This lesson will help you to:
- understand the importance of grammar, spelling and punctuation
- practise identifying the skills.

Grammar, spelling and punctuation

In your test you have to use correct grammar, including subject-verb agreement and correct, consistent use of tense. You also have to use accurate punctuation and spelling and ensure that the meaning is clear.

Here is some writing which gives information and opinion about a family holiday. This document could be called a report. Read the report then look at the annotations. These give you information about grammar, spelling and punctuation.

Key terms

Subject means:
- what the sentence is about
- the person or thing which is doing (or being) the action in the sentence.

Agreement means: the subject and the verb have the correct tense and number and fit together, for example: _John enjoyed_ his holiday in Scotland. _One person_ did something _in the past._ _John_ and _Peter_ _are_ now back in school. _Two people_ are doing something _in the present._

> subject and verb agree

> list separated with commas, correct spelling

> subject-verb agreement, correct change of tense

> subject-verb agreement, correct use of tense

> subject-verb agreement, correct use of tense

> acceptable and effective one-word sentence, use of exclamation mark

> uses 'and' instead of full stop

Turkey is a great place. Our hotel had a swimming pool, tennis court, outdoor pool table and barbeque. We all had a good time which was a surprise because my Dad doesn't like too much sun. He spent a lot of his time looking in museums. Boring! I just like to relax by the pool when I'm on holiday and my Mum loves to sunbathe.

Activity 1

Below is a piece of writing that gives some information, description and opinion about *The Hobbit*. It might be part of a document we would call a book review. Read the text and complete the tasks below it.

> *The Hobbit* is an excellent book. I read it many years ago and it remains one of my all-time favourites. The book has great characters, fantasy, adventure and lots of drama. I liked Gandalf best when I first read it because of his magical powers, but now I think Bilbo really is the hero. There are lots of brilliant characters. Gollum is great! Are you looking for a good book to read? I would definitely recommend this book to you.

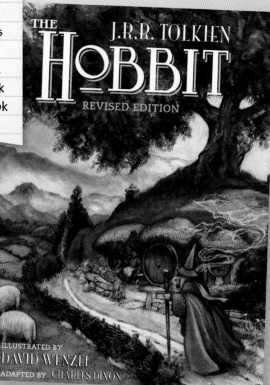

1 Find and write down examples of the following grammar from the text:
   a subject-verb agreement in the present tense
   b subject-verb agreement in the past tense
   c two examples of a change of tense
   d use of commas in a list
   e an example of a *doing* verb and a *being* verb from the same sentence
   f three different sorts of punctuation
   g some words which are difficult to spell correctly.

Peer/Self-assessment activity

In this chapter you have learned and practised some skills to do with being able to write at Level 1. Before you do a short test, think about the work you have been doing and how confident you are about what you have learned. Then tick the boxes which are closest to how you feel.

Skill	Not confident	Need some more support	Very confident
I understand what a document is and how documents have different purposes.			
I understand how to write clearly, coherently and with appropriate detail.			
I know how to present information in a logical sequence.			
I understand how to use language, format and structure.			
I understand how to improve my grammar, spelling and punctuation.			

How to fill in your renewal driving licence application form

Driving Licence Renewal Application

D46P

Number is:

...e it and quote it in any correspondence with the

Your health

...ust fill in either Part A or Part B, or we will sen
...pplication back to you.

...have already told us about a medical condition that c...
... your fitness to drive – and you have no new medical
...tion – miss out Part A and go on to Part B of this secti...

...A

... you ever had, or do you currently suffer from,
... of the following conditions?   No ☐   Yes

...ou have answered 'Yes', please tick all the appropriate boxes.

. Epilepsy
2. Fits or blackouts
3. Repeated attacks of sudden disabling giddiness
4. Diabetes controlled by insulin
5. Diabetes controlled by tablets
6. An implanted cardiac pacemaker
7. An implanted cardiac defibrillator (ICD)
8. Angina (heart pain) which is easily brought on by driving
9. Persistent alcohol misuse or dependency
10. Persistent drug misuse or dependency
11. Parkinson's disease
12. Narcolepsy or sleep apnoea syndrome
13. Stroke, with any symptoms lasting longer than one month recurrent "mini-strokes" or TIAs

Level 1 mini Writing test

Now use what you have learned to do the test that follows. Answer **both** of the questions in 45 minutes. One of the questions is focused on providing information and the second question asks for ideas and opinions.

The focuses for this test are to:
- write clearly and coherently, including an appropriate level of detail
- present information in a logical sequence
- use language, format and structure suitable for audience and purpose
- use correct grammar, including correct and consistent use of tense
- ensure written work includes accurate punctuation and spelling and that meaning is clear.

Question 1

There are many more cyclists than there used to be and lots of bikes are stolen every day. Write a leaflet for bike owners informing them of the best ways to keep their bike safe. Tell them about:
- the risk of having their bike stolen
- how to keep their bike safe at home
- ways to make a bike secure
- insurance for their bike.

Remember to:
- write a plan for your leaflet
- write to inform
- keep your audience in mind
- write in sentences
- use paragraphs.

Question 2

There is some money available from your town council to spend on providing things for young people to do. Write a letter to your local councillor putting forward your ideas on how this money should be spent. Tell the councillor about:
- the need for more amenities for young people
- some possible ideas for spending the money
- the idea you think is best
- how your ideas would benefit young people.

Remember to:
- plan your answer
- write a formal business letter
- give your ideas and opinions
- keep your audience in mind
- keep in mind the purpose of the letter.

TestZone

Student sample answers

Here are three student responses to the test on writing a leaflet (question 1, page 73). Read the answers together with the examiner comments around and after the answers. First, remind yourself of the question (page 73).

Student A   *Pass* ✓

> There can be a high risk of your bike being stolen if you do not chain it up at the shops or at home especially if it is a very valuable bike. ✓ You should always make sure your bike is secure even if your just gone for five minutes, it's still enough time for a theif to jump on your bike and ride off. ✓
>
> At home you should also keep it chained up or in a shed/garage because if a theif walks past your house there is a high risk of them grabing it and riding away. ✓
>
> You can prevent this by buying a bike lock or a shed to put in your back garden, even if you live in a flat you could bring it inside safe. ✓ With some bikes you can easily remove a wheel to make it imobile, these are good. ✓ But the best thing to have is insurance so that if your bike is stolen you can get a new one. ✓ If you do not do these things you may have to spend a lot of money getting a new bike. ✓

Topic clearly stated, mentions 'risk'; good sentence.

Informs/advises, develops topic: two spelling errors.

Develops information/advice, sequencing evident.

Develops ideas, follows the suggested scaffolding.

Relevant information develops the writing.

Follows the suggestion in the scaffolding, could be expanded.

Appropriate concluding remark.

Examiner comment

The student has understood the task clearly and written a well-sequenced piece in an appropriate register. There is room for development of ideas but the topic is covered. The sentence structure is secure and the concluding remark is telling. For content, the mark is just in Band 3 with five marks, and for accuracy the mark is three. An overall mark of 8/10 would achieve Level 1.

Student B *Borderline* ✓✗

Are your bikes being stolen, or do you not know where to put it when your not riding it. Well, a few tips might do you some good. ✓

> Rhetorical question is valid and subject matter introduced. Missing question mark.

If you've just got a new bike and you might be scared of it being stolen then get a chain and a padlock and your sorted, But what if you don't have a chain and a padlock. ✓ Well, have you got a shed, porch or even a conservetry. ✓ Then put it in there when your not riding it. ✓ If you have non of these then bring it into your home and try not to make a mess. ✓

> Valid suggestion made; inappropriate colloquialism; incorrect punctuation.

> Spelling error, missing question mark.

> The two simple sentences should have been combined.

Is your bike a bit lose and wobberly, then do not attept to ride it untill fixed either get tools and learn from a friend or take it to a bike shop. ✗

> Valid ideas related to topic.

> The idea is inappropriate to the task set which is about stolen bikes. Spelling errors and weak sentence structure.

Examiner comment

The student has presented two suggestions for making a bicycle secure: padlocking it or moving it indoors. The task has been understood. However, some of the ideas do not relate to the focus of the question. There are punctuation and spelling errors but also evidence of correct sentence structure.

The mark for content is Band 2 with a mark of three. The accuracy mark is Band 2 with a mark of three.

The mark of 6/10 would be a borderline Level 1.

TestZone

If your bikes gets stolen theres a lot that Could happen might not get it back or Someone could get run over when there on it. ✓ This person that this leaflet is written for didn't get his bike back but he got some money for insurance . ✓

> Some remarks made on the topic, weak sentence structure and spelling errors.

> Some confusion about the 'person' and the 'for insurance' should be 'from'.

Examiner comment

The student offers only a brief and limited response to the question, noting the issue but presenting some irrelevant and confused ideas. There are errors in accuracy but some evidence of secure sentence structure. Content: Band 1 with a mark of two; accuracy: Band 1 with a mark of two.

Overall 4/10 does not achieve Level 1.

Peer/Self-assessment activity

Question 1

1   Compare the answers you and you partner wrote with the student who gained a mark above Level 2 (Student A). Discuss the following points with your partner:
    ▶ How many informing or advising ideas did you each have for question 1?
    ▶ Did you follow the scaffolding suggested in the question?

Question 2

2   Re-read the leaflet by Student B. This student was close to getting a Level 2.
    ▶ In Student B's writing, how would you improve sentences 3, 4 and 5?
    ▶ Student B was given a low mark for the content of their writing. Discuss and write down what they should have done to improve it.

3   Find some examples of good sentences in your report.
    ▶ What kind of sentences are the best ones? Why do you think they are good?
    ▶ With your partner, find one example of a simple, compound and complex sentence in each other's work.
    ▶ Student C was given a very low mark for the content of their report. Discuss with your partner why you think this was. What should they have done?

4   The first task was to inform but you can see that the 'information' sometimes looks like advice. Find the parts of your letter, and your partner's letter, which you think are informative and the parts which give advice.
    ▶ Which words, ideas and phrases are giving advice?
    ▶ Write down ways you could have been more informative.

Skill standard

Take full part in formal and informal discussions and exchanges that include unfamiliar subjects.

What you need to do:

▶ Make relevant and extended contributions to discussions, allowing for and responding to others' input.

▶ Prepare for and contribute to the formal discussion of ideas and opinions.

▶ Make different kinds of contributions to discussions.

▶ Present information/points of view clearly and in appropriate language.

Your teacher or tutor will help you to decide whether to use the following tasks. They will also help you to organise the tasks should you attempt them.

Task 1: Discussion

Imagine a group of you are planning a weekend trip to a music festival or similar event. You would need to organise:

▶ transport to the event

▶ obtaining tickets

▶ food and equipment for camping

▶ who is in charge of what

▶ cost.

Discuss these issues in your group. You could use an actual local event to plan around if you like.

Task 2: Discussion

In a group, discuss the advantages and disadvantages of part-time jobs. You can use your own experience or things you have heard about as material for your input into the discussion.

Here's a starting point:

You might be getting paid some useful pocket money; but are you being exploited?

My learning ▶

This lesson will help you to:
● understand what documents are
● understand the various purposes for documents.

Understand what documents are

Documents

In your test you will be asked to create at least one piece of writing (which the skill standard refers to as 'documents'). In your daily life you are surrounded by documents. There are many different sorts of document, such as:

application forms	books	pamphlets	leaflets
notices	greetings cards	emails	recipes
brochures	personal letters	text messages	reports
reviews	licenses	business letters	magazines
articles	newspapers	notes	

In your test you will be writing documents to communicate with others. Their purpose will be to convey something, such as information, ideas, opinions, requests and so on.

You will need to be clear what sort of documents you are being asked to write and for what purpose. The Writing tasks you are set will tell you this. Each Writing question will give you guidance about the type of document required and its purpose. You should read the Writing questions carefully.

Activity 1

1 Match the writing purpose to the document type. The first one has been done for you. The others are mixed up.

Purpose		Document type
1 Writing to make a point about poor service at a restaurant	→	A Formal letter of complaint
2 Writing about the local flower show to give out to passers-by		B Review
3 Writing to tell people how good a new hair product is		C Instruction sheet
4 Writing about the dangers of global warming for your college magazine		D Handout
5 Writing to tell people about the work of a charity		E Application form
6 Writing about a book you have read and recommend to others		F Article
7 Writing about how to build a flat-pack bookshelf		G Advertisement
8 Writing to ask to join the local golf club		H Report
9 Writing about your school hockey match for a local paper		I Letter of application
10 Writing to apply for a passport		J Information leaflet

2 Work with a partner and make a list of documents you have come across in the last few days. The types of document mentioned so far in this lesson will help you. Use a table like this one.

The document	Where you came across it	Its purpose

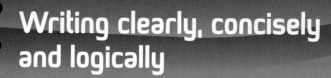

My learning objectives ▶

This lesson will help you to:
- understand what writing to inform clearly, concisely and logically means.

Writing clearly, concisely and logically

Writing clearly and concisely

It is important to make sure your reader is not confused by what you write. You are not writing to make your reader feel lost or to have to dig around to find your meaning. You want to give information and perhaps advice and good sense in a functional way. If you keep this in mind, you will write **clearly** and **concisely**.

Your writing will have a distinct purpose or function, and presenting information concisely is an important part of being functional.

Key terms

Clearly means:
- easy to understand
- explicit
- to the point
- not muddled
- obvious
- plain
- unmistakable
- not made difficult
- uncomplicated
- not confused.

Concisely means:
- briefly
- in a compact way
- to the point
- not wasting words
- staying on the subject
- condensed
- selective
- writing the important things.

Activity 1

Look at these two images, then answer the questions below.

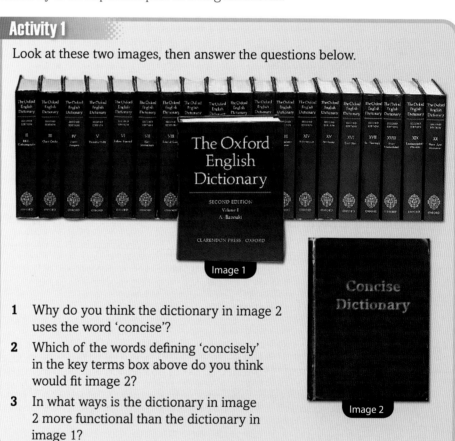

Image 1

Image 2

1 Why do you think the dictionary in image 2 uses the word 'concise'?

2 Which of the words defining 'concisely' in the key terms box above do you think would fit image 2?

3 In what ways is the dictionary in image 2 more functional than the dictionary in image 1?

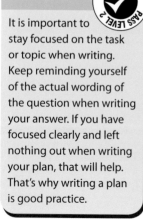

It is important to stay focused on the task or topic when writing. Keep reminding yourself of the actual wording of the question when writing your answer. If you have focused clearly and left nothing out when writing your plan, that will help. That's why writing a plan is good practice.

Writing logically

It is important that you write **logically** so that what you write makes sense to the reader. Whatever kind of document you have to compose, it needs to be well-organised, and the information (as well as ideas and opinions) must link together and be clearly related to the task or topic.

Key term

Logically means:
- **in an orderly way**
- **in a relevant way**
- **un-muddled**
- **well-organised**
- **clearly related**
- **fitting**
- **making points in sequence**
- **following after**
- **connecting**
- **linking together.**

Activity 2

Look at these two images, then answer the questions below.

One of these images represents a chess game. The other represents a Sudoku puzzle. You may need to discuss or find out how the game of chess and Sudoku puzzles work.

1   In what ways does the game of chess rely on being played in a logical way?
2   What is logical about a Sudoku puzzle?
3   Find some words in the key term box above which fit the activities of chess and Sudoku.

My learning objectives ▶

This lesson will help you to:
● understand what writing information on complex subjects means.

Writing information on complex subjects

You will be expected to write on *complex subjects*. This means subjects where there might be:

▶ quite a lot of detail

▶ more than one thing to think about

▶ some facts and figures to consider

▶ some general and some specific information

▶ various aspects to the information

▶ some things that may be more important than others

▶ some advice

▶ dos and don'ts

… all as part of the information.

A well-written complex text will be easy to understand if the writer has organised the information clearly and logically. This needs thought and planning. The writer will also have kept to the point and selected only the information they need; they will have been concise. This also needs thought and planning. A complex piece of information does not need to be very long but it does have to be well-planned.

> **PASS LEVEL 2** ✓
>
> When you write a plan, use lists and bullet points, diagrams and brief notes. Don't write in full because it takes up time. When you write an answer, you will need to use continuous writing to show how you can write in sentences and paragraphs.

Activity 1

Opposite is a text that provides information. It is part of a leaflet published by National Rail entitled 'Rail travel made easy'.

This could be described as a complex text, but also one which is clear, concise and logical.

Read the text carefully, then write notes in response to tasks 1 and 2 below. You might want to work with a partner.

1   Complexity

   a   How many different pieces of specific information are there in the section 'Help us to help you'? Write them down as a list.

   b   How many different pieces of specific information are there in the section 'Wheelchairs'? Write them down as a list.

   c   Write down some general information from each section.

   d   Write down what you think is the most important information in the text.

2   Clear, concise, logical

   a   Which of the 'clear' words from the key terms box on page 80 apply to the text? Try to explain your choices.

   b   See if you can find any wasted words, or words going off the point in the text.

   c   Look back at what you learned about writing logically. What is the evidence for this in the text? Use some of the 'logically' words from the key term box on page 81 in your notes.

Notice how this text is written in prose (in full sentences and paragraphs) but it could have been written partly as a bullet-point list.

3   Rewrite the text using some bullet points. Keep the two sections. Make sure your list covers everything.

Rail travel made easy

■ Help us to help you

Do make your needs known to us. Rail staff are trained to give you assistance so please tell them if you are likely to require help getting on and off trains or receiving information. This will enable us to help you if disruption affects your journey.

There are limits to the amount of assistance we can provide. We cannot escort customers throughout the whole of their journey, neither can we provide personal care (for example, help with eating and drinking, taking medication or using the toilet) or carry heavy luggage.

■ Wheelchairs

Most trains can accommodate wheelchairs that are within the dimensions given in government public transport regulations (700mm wide, 1200mm long). There are a small number of older trains that can only currently carry wheelchairs that have a maximum width of 670mm.

The maximum combined weight of a person and their wheelchair that can be conveyed is limited by two things: the capabilities of the individual member of staff assisting the passenger and the stated maximum safe working load of the ramp (between 230kg and 300kg).

There are a limited number of spaces available to wheelchair users on each train so, where reservations apply, we recommend that you book your space in advance.

Peer/Self-assessment activity

In this chapter you have learned and practised some skills to do with being able to write at Level 2. Before you do a short test, think about the work you have been doing and how confident you are about what you have learned. Then tick the boxes which are closest to how you feel.

Skill	Not confident	Need some more support	Very confident
I understand what a document is and how documents have different purposes.			
I understand how to write information clearly, concisely and logically.			
I know how to present information on complex subjects concisely and clearly.			

Level 2 mini Writing test

Now use what you have learned to respond to this question, which asks you to write with some complexity.

You recently attended the final of a sporting event between two local teams with a history of rivalry. Write a report for your school or college magazine about the closely fought match you saw and which team eventually lifted the trophy.

Remember to:
* write a plan
* focus on presenting complex information clearly
* write in sentences and paragraphs.

Student sample answers

Here are three student responses to the question on writing a report (page 85). Read the answers together with the examiner comments around and after the answers. First, remind yourself of the question (page 85).

Student A *Pass* ✓

Match report
RMAC vs. ALL Saints
On Saturday 28th April was the football trophy final between RMAC and All Saints School. ✓ The last time these two teams challenged each other it involved a major incident where one boy had to be taken to hospital. ✓ Luckily this match went much more smoothly although the rivalry was just as strong. ✓ RMAC scored a goal in the first few minutes which got the All Saints team in a bit of a bad mood. ✓ All Saints aggressive fight to score was unfortunately unsuccessful as RMAC kept their chances at bay with their excellent defenders. ✓ After a while All Saints managed to score making the teams even. They scored again after a few more minutes which lightened their mood considerably. ✓

After a time of end to end play RMAC managed to equalise. Then after some vigorous play by both sides which resulted in a foul we were treated to the drama of a penalty which All Saints failed to convert. ✓ The miss was costly because RMAC grabbed the glory in the dying minutes. ✓

It has been a while since RMAC won the trophy and judging by their performance in this game they certainly put in the hard effort to deserve it. ✓ A team player from Budmouth who won the cup two years in a row, presented the trophy ✓

Examiner comments:
- Information given; straightforward sentence could be better arranged.
- Develops information and ideas
- Reporting; develops.
- Reporting; some humour.
- Appropriate register; complex sentence; technically accurate; missing apostrophe.
- Reference back to 'mood' shows good sequencing.
- Some appropriate reportage phrases used.
- Appropriate reportage register concluding the paragraph.
- Summary of the history of the team, appropriate comments.
- Some appropriate reportage phrases used.

Examiner comment

The student has understood the task well. An appropriate register for a sports report has been adopted with success. The writing is clear and appropriate. Perhaps the piece could have been extended but most of the requirements of the mark scheme for Band 3 have been achieved. The mark would be seven for content. The writing is accurate with well organised paragraphs. The accuracy mark is five. A total of 12/15 would achieve Level 2.

Student B *Borderline* ✓✗

As you no it's the football final between Weymouth and Dorchester and is definatly a grudge match. ✓ The game got going with Weymouth going forward but they never took the chance to score. ✓ There were some hard tackles but on both sides the players were fair and by half time it was a draw. ✓ When weymouth scored in the second half early there was great disapointment for the Dorchester fans and they thought they were bound to loose. ✓

But then a great cross from James made it a draw when Jackson put it in the net. ✓ Dorchester were on top and in the second half were dominant. ✓ The weymouth players getting rattled and fouling all the time gave Dorchester a penalty near the end. ✓ It was tense and the crowd didn't want to look. ✓ It went in and Dorchester won the trophy for the first time ever. ✓

From your football reporter Josh Scott. ✓

> Introduces topic, spelling errors −'no' and 'definatly'.

> Develops report, some weak expression.

> Develops report, some weak construction.

> Further development with missing capital letter, spelling errors, weak construction.

> Valid link but to a new paragraph; effective sentence; good sequencing.

> Rather weak last phrase.

> Effective short sentence.

> Develops report, missing capital letter and commas.

> Valid sentence but 'It went in' a weak phrase.

> Valid signing off, missing comma.

Examiner comment

The reader gets the sense of the game from the report and there is some development. Expression and construction are often secure but with definite weaknesses. Some information is imparted. The writing is in Band 2 of the mark scheme with a mark of five and an accuracy mark of four from Band 2.

Overall a mark of 9/15 would be borderline. The student would need to show some general improvement to ensure a Level 2 mark in future.

TestZone

Student C *Fail* X

Well they walked on the pitch and you new it was gonna be trouble from the warm up when the players were eyeballing each other and the fans shouting, ✓ Weymouth terras was playing at home so as you can imagen there was lots of weymouth supportes but that didn't stop the Dorch supporters making a lot of noise. ✓ At the half way mark it was 0-0 and nothing really happened through the game but within a few mins left of the game terras got tired which gave dorch a chance to have a break through. ✓ They took it with both hands on and there new player headed into the net. ✓ That made the terras give up and Dorchester won 1-0 they had won the trophy! what a game for a schoolboy team. ✓ There supporters carried on cheering till the terras went home. ✓

- Sets the scene, spelling errors, weak opening and structure.
- Weak sentence structure, spelling errors, grammatical errors, some development of atmosphere.
- Some reporting here but unhelpful abbreviations and weak structure.
- Good sentence but weak expression and spelling error.
- Missing punctuation and capital letter.
- Valid conclusion.

Examiner comment

Some aspects of the task have been fulfilled. Some reporting of the occasion is achieved. However, there are no real introductory or explanatory aspects to the writing. There are numerous errors in sentence structure, spelling and grammar with limited development of the actual report. Content is Band 2 with a mark of four; accuracy is band 1 with a mark of two. Overall a mark of 6/15 would not achieve Level 2.

Peer/Self-assessment activity

1 Compare the answer you and your partner wrote with the student who gained a mark above Level 2 (Student A). Discuss the following points with your partner:
   - Did you write a title or heading for your match report?
   - Did you use any interesting words or phrases which sports reporters sometimes use, like Student A, sentence 9?

2 The task was to inform by reporting an event. Find the parts of your report, and your partner's report, which you think are informative.
   - Which words, ideas and phrases are reporting what was going on?
   - Write down ways you could have been more informative, or more like a reporter.

3 Re-read the report by Student B. This student was close to getting a Level 2.
   - In Student B's writing, how would you improve sentences 2 and 3?
   - Think of a good, 'sports report' headline for Student B's report and write it down.

4 With your partner, find examples of correct subject-verb agreement and correct uses of tense in each other's work.
   - What kind of sentences are the best ones? Why do you think they are good?
   - With your partner, find one example of a simple, compound and complex sentence in each other's work.
   - Student C was given a very low mark for the accuracy of their report. Discuss with your partner why you think this was. What should they have done?

Level 2 Speaking, Listening and Communication tasks

Skill standard

Make a range of contributions to discussions and in a range of contexts, including those that are unfamiliar, and make effective presentations.

What you need to do:

▶ Consider complex information and give a relevant, cogent response in appropriate language.

▶ Present information and ideas clearly and persuasively to others.

▶ Adapt contributions to suit audience, purpose and situation.

▶ Make significant contributions to discussions, taking a range of roles and helping to move discussion forward.

Your teacher or tutor will help you to decide whether to use the following task. They will also help you to organise the task should you attempt it.

Task: Presentation

Here is a topic for an effective presentation: Life for people who have disabilities or impairments is much better than it was years ago. But there is more that needs to be done.

You will need to do some research to provide material. Your aim is to present information and ideas clearly and to persuade your audience.

Your audience will be members of your class and your teacher or tutor.

Here is a brainstorm of suggestions to help your preparation. You need to choose from these; you won't have time to do them all.

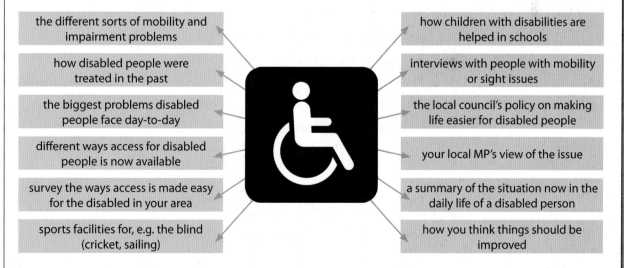

the different sorts of mobility and impairment problems

how disabled people were treated in the past

the biggest problems disabled people face day-to-day

different ways access for disabled people is now available

survey the ways access is made easy for the disabled in your area

sports facilities for, e.g. the blind (cricket, sailing)

how children with disabilities are helped in schools

interviews with people with mobility or sight issues

the local council's policy on making life easier for disabled people

your local MP's view of the issue

a summary of the situation now in the daily life of a disabled person

how you think things should be improved

You might open your views to a discussion with three or four members of your class, but the task is to produce a *persuasive individual presentation*.

My learning ▶

This lesson will help you to:
● understand what writing to persuade means
● understand what persuasive writing in advertising means.

Persuasive writing in advertisements

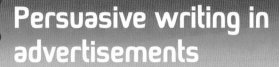

One of the most obvious and common everyday forms of persuasion is advertising. Here are two very different advertisements.

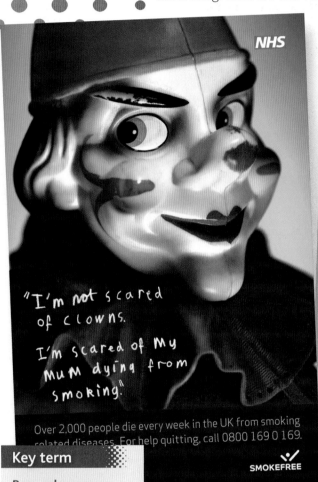

The first advertisement is intended to shock. It uses a frightening image and harsh language to influence the reader and win them over to stop smoking.

The second advertisement uses a softer, cosier image of a puppy to entice or coax people to buy the product.

Activity 1

Here is another advertisement which tries to persuade.

Cadbury Dairy Milk Buttons: our little bags of fun turn fifty and Fairtrade

> When you write to persuade – whatever the document is – try to keep in mind that you are doing something very similar to an advertisement. You are advertising yourself, or your point of view or an idea you have.

Look at the image carefully and then note down some responses to the questions below.

1 What is the advertisement trying to get you to buy?

2 What are the images of the bags of chocolate buttons and the Fairtrade symbol suggesting in the Cadbury's advertisement?

3 Which of the words defining 'persuade' in the key term box on page 90 best fits the advertisement?

4 The advertisements on page 90 were described as 'shocking' and 'cosy'. Think of some words to describe the Cadbury's Buttons advertisement.

5 With a partner, discuss your favourite advertisements.

   a Why do you like them?

   b What is persuasive about them?

What you are concerned with is *functional* writing: writing that will have a specific purpose and result. Advertisements are very functional because they have a focused purpose and effect.

There are many other sorts of persuasive writing, as these examples show.

Letters or emails to:

▶ get something put right

▶ get a friend to do something

▶ try and get something changed locally

▶ try and get something achieved nationally

▶ congratulate or complain and get a result.

Articles for newspapers or magazines to:

▶ express a point of view and hope to influence others

▶ point out something that is wrong and how it can be put right

▶ tell people about something good and why you think so.

My learning objectives ▶

This lesson will help you to:
- understand what writing to persuade means
- understand what persuasive writing in letters means.

Persuasive writing in letters

Opposite is a letter with some annotations. It is an example of a piece of functional, persuasive writing. Read the letter, together with the annotations, then complete the activity below.

Activity 1

1   The letter uses some deliberately persuasive words and phrases meant to *win over*, *coax* and *influence* the reader. Some have been underlined in each paragraph to start you off. Write out some more winning words and phrases from each paragraph.

2   Write the paragraph plan that would go with this letter. Include the main points and the key words. Use the ideas from the boxes opposite but in your own words.

Formal, business-letter frame

Cleveholm Community Centre Project

23 Forest Street

Cleveholm

Lancs

The National Lottery Funding Agency

Holborn

London

Dear Sir,

We wish to apply for a grant of £100,000 to build a community centre in our village.

The community centre would be a <u>wonderful</u> facility for <u>all ages</u> in our community. At the moment, there is nowhere for the older generation to <u>spend time together</u> in a <u>sociable way</u>. Many of the older generation live alone and have little to <u>interest them in life</u>. A community centre would lift their spirits and give them purpose; they would also be able to benefit others by organising charity events, holding coffee mornings, reading clubs and so on. <u>The centre would be a daily beacon of light for many people</u>.

<u>Furthermore</u>, we would envisage that in the evenings the Centre would become a thriving youth club with indoor sporting, music and film activities for the young people of the village. This would give them a purpose, keep them off the streets and mean that they did not need to travel to town for entertainment. At present there is little to do for young people in Cleveholm.

<u>Everybody</u> is in favour of this project. We have over 2,000 signatures on our petition.

We <u>hope</u> you will be persuaded to grant us the money. We are able to provide you with detailed and convincing plans should you, as we <u>hope</u>, wish to proceed.

Yours faithfully,

George Bentley,

Secretary, Cleveholm Community Centre Project

Annotations:

- Clear statement of purpose
- Brings in the wider community to sway, or bring round the reader
- Persuasive link word
- Develops persuasive, convincing reasons
- Concludes using persuasive words
- Persuasive points and words to influence the reader
- Uses emotional language
- Develops, adds more ideas related to the purpose
- Shows level of support

My learning objectives ▶

This lesson will help you to:
- understand what a range of different writing styles means
- practise responding to a range of different writing styles.

Writing in a range of different styles

The style of your writing will depend on the audience and purpose of your writing. Your writing will mainly be concerned with informing and persuading in a functional way.

You may have heard people talk about formal and informal style and this is a useful start.

The style may be *formal*:

correct	approved	conventional	standard English
proper	official	straightforward	businesslike…

Or it might be *informal*:

colloquial	slang	casual	easy-going
relaxed	unofficial	natural	

Writing style is about the tone you adopt for different purposes, and is connected to the *register* you use.

Here are some words to describe just some of the different tones which writers use:

light-hearted	solemn	serious	reflective	flippant
cynical	detached	emotional	tear-jerking	humorous
factual	emotive	exciting	threatening	committed
polite	impolite	subjective	objective	respectful
lively	colloquial			

The letter on page 93 is a formal letter, but you could also use other words to describe the style in which it is written:

▶ In parts, the letter is serious, factual, polite and emotive because these aspects of style help the writer achieve what they want.

▶ The letter is not threatening, cynical or impolite in its style because that would not have fitted the purpose or the audience.

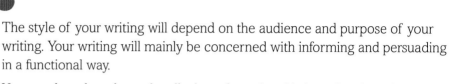

Cleveholm Community Centre Project
23 Forest Street
Cleveholm
Lancs

The National Lottery Funding Agency
Holborn
London

Dear Sir,

We wish to apply for a grant of £100,000 to build a community centre in our village.

The community centre would be a _wonderful_ facility for _all ages_ in our community. At the moment, there is nowhere for the older generation to spend time together in a _sociable way_. Many of the older generation are lonely and have little to _interest them in life_. A com... to lift their spirits and give them... to benefit others by...

Activity 1

1   Here are some short pieces of writing.
    For each one:
    - write down the purpose (inform or persuade)
    - decide which formal or informal words describe each piece
    - choose some of the tone words from the suggestions on page 94 to describe the style in which the pieces are written
    - suggest who the audience might be.

> In an examination situation, like your Writing test, you should rarely – almost never – write informally. It's much better to play it safe. So look again at the 'formal' words on page 94 and remember them.

Text A

Ballooning is great fun – in fact it's a gas! Admittedly, you have to get up at four in the morning and stand around freezing to death while a bunch of geeks get the thing filled with air, but the adrenalin rush as you ascend above the city is awesome. And it's so quiet up there … eerie … weird … great. Try it – and change your life!

Text B

You can smell the Stoeung Meanchey rubbish dump long before you reach it. Unbelievably, this is home to hundreds of adults and children who scavenge a living from the rubbish. Across this towering nightmare, tiny figures pick through the filth, day and night, for anything they can recycle and sell. If they don't find anything, they don't eat.

Text C

Dear Sir,

I think you should know that, unless I receive immediate reimbursement for the money I spent renting what you have the audacity to call a holiday cottage, I shall be contacting my solicitor.

Yours etc.

Gerald Tufton

Text D

In the Reds' 4–1 mauling at home by in-form opponents, the only consolation was the 30-yarder by hotshot Harwood. The battling spirit of recent home games had clearly deserted them and the fans were denied three points. The visitors, meanwhile, were over the moon.

2   For each piece of writing, list the key words and phrases used by the writers which helped you to decide on the style.

3   Try to explain how the words are effective.

My learning objectives ▶

This lesson will help you to:
- Understand what simple, compound and complex sentences are
- Practise identifying different sentence types.

Sentence structures

Understanding simple, compound and complex sentences

There are three different kinds of sentence that you need to know about:

▶ simple sentences

▶ compound sentences

▶ complex sentences.

You use these now when you write, it's just that you probably don't know you're doing it! You really do need to know what these different types of sentences are, so here are some examples:

Simple sentences

These are made up of just one **clause**. They must contain a **subject** and a **verb**. For example:

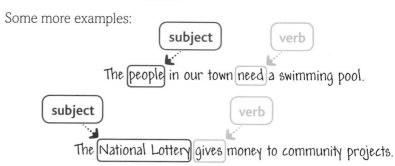

Some more examples:

The people in our town need a swimming pool.

The National Lottery gives money to community projects.

Compound sentences

These are made up of two simple sentences (or clauses) joined together using linking words like 'and' or 'but'. For example:

simple sentence   simple sentence

I am writing to you about the town I live in.   +   I hope you will read my letter.

↓

I am writing to you about the town I live in **and** I hope you will read my letter.

compound sentence

> **Key term**
>
> **Clause**
> A group of words that has a complete verb, i.e. 'I flew a kite' = one clause.
>
> **Subject**
> A word or group of words that tell you what the sentence is about.
>
> **Verb**
> Verbs are words that represent actions (to run), speech (to say) or the senses (to think).

Activity 1

Make compound sentences by joining the simple sentences below with the linking words 'or', 'but' or 'and'.

1 I like running. I would rather go swimming.
2 David could spend his pocket money now. He could save it for a rainy day.
3 The National Lottery has to make difficult decisions. All the people of our town hope you will give us a grant.

Complex sentences

These are made up of a main clause, which can stand on its own because it expresses a complete thought, and one or more subordinate clauses, which do not make sense on their own. For example:

main clause   subordinate clause

We need a swimming pool in our town | which everybody will be able to enjoy.

Activity 2

Match the main clauses with the correct subordinate clauses.

Main clause	Subordinate clause
1 I decided it was time to tidy my bedroom	A since I started swimming regularly.
2 We could go to the cinema this afternoon	B unless you hurry up.
3 I feel much healthier	C although it is a nice day outside.
4 Jo refused to talk to me	D when I couldn't open my wardrobe door.
5 You're going to be really late	E until I apologised.

Activity 3

1 What sort of sentence is each of the following? Explain your answer by writing out the sentences and labelling the clauses, as has been shown in the examples on pages 96–97.

   a The dog barked loudly.

   b Many people like learning about sentences because writing is improved by having interesting sentences.

   c We are looking forward to the exams although it's going to be hard work.

   d I left the party early and I caught the last bus home.

   e The dog barked loudly when we left the house, though we did go quietly.

   f Most of us in the class have learned something about sentences.

2 Imagine you are the person at The National Lottery who decides where the money goes.

   ● Write a short letter in reply to the request for the funding of a community swimming pool.

   ● Use at least one simple, one compound and one complex sentence in your letter.

Peer/Self-assessment activity

In this chapter you have learned and practised some skills to do with being able to write at Level 2. Before you do a short test, think about the work you have been doing and how confident you are about what you have learned. Then tick the boxes which are closest to how you feel.

Skill	Not confident	Need some more support	Very confident
I understand what writing to persuade means.			
I understand what writing in different styles for different purposes means.			
I understand what simple, compound and complex sentences are and how to use them.			

Level 2 mini Writing test

In this test you need to apply what you have learned in this chapter.

For one of your birthday presents you have been given two vouchers to do a parachute jump. This includes a day's training, equipment and the actual jump. You want a friend to go with you.

Write a letter to a friend persuading them to join you in this adventure.

Remember to:

- be persuasive
- think about choosing the most appropriate writing style, register and tone (you could mix informality, formality, humour, etc. in a letter to a friend)
- be aware of the way you construct sentences

Hint: complex sentences can be interesting and compelling but short, sharp, simple sentences can also be very effective.

Student sample answers

Here are three student responses to the Writing test on page 99. Read the answers together with the examiner comments. First, remind yourself of the task (page 99).

Student A Pass ✓

> Salutation is fine but lacks comma.

> Address is evident as part of a letter frame

28 Bexley Street
✓ Oxford

> Good opening sentence, fluent, succinct, good vocabulary.

Dear Sophie ✓
I would be delighted if you would join me to go parachute jumping for my birthday. ✓ Everything is paid for as I recieved two vouchers off my aunty Jean for my birthday present. ✓ The day includes training, equipment and the actual jump. The training will be with professionals. ✓

> Information clearly expressed, common spelling error.

> Ideas clearly expressed, effective short sentences, spelling error.

It will be amazing learning how to parachute jump, you could use this in later life or even become our hobbie! ✓ What a thrill it will be jumping out of a plane being so close to death, your heart beating so fast it feels like its going to jump out of your chest. ✓ Then when you pull the trigger and you know your safe but you can't help your pulse rising in excitement. ✓

> Spelling error – 'hobbie'

> Persuasive words and ideas, appropriate use of exclamation mark.

> Sophisticated construction, reflective, persuasive, good use of tense, 'its' error.

I have chosen you because I know you love action and doing dangerous things and because you are a good friend and always there for me. ✓ Doing this will make our friendship, knowing we can trust each other. ✓ Doing this together will be the greatest achievement of our lives and all our friends will be so jelous that we went and they didn't. Just imagine the look on their faces. Well, hope to hear from you soon. Please say you'll come. ✓
Lots of love
Holly ✓

> Evocative and persuasive ideas, vivid image created, valid and effective use of conjunction to begin the sentence; the construction is not quite right, spelling error – 'your'.

> Links personal persuasion with the scaffolding idea, spelling error.

> Informal but valid sign off

> Effective change of tone; persuasive, ends on a cliché.

> Develops personal persuasion, emotive content.

> Rounded, valid and effective conclusion.

Examiner comment

The letter shows evidence of a letter frame; the register mixes formality and informality successfully and appropriately. Ideas are communicated with clarity and success. Material is organised. Complex ideas and images are evoked. Clearly addresses the audience in a persuasive and engaging way. Sentences are varied and constructed to enhance meaning. Secure grammar. A few spelling errors. The writing is Band 3 for content with a mark of eight and Band 3 for accuracy with a mark of five. The overall mark of 13/15 would achieve Level 2.

Student B *Borderline* ✓✗

No address attempted, which is required even in an informal letter to a friend; informal salutation lacks punctuation.

Basic information clear.

Purpose of letter clear, missing apostrophe.

Further information given; weak expression.

Attempt to persuade; missing apostrophe.

Friend directly addressed; persuasive idea; compounded sentences.

Hey Carry ✓

For my birthday my mum bought me two vouchers to go parachute jumping. ✓ Im allowed to take a friend and I was wondering if you would like to come with me. ✓ Everything is paid for, so you wont need any money or nothing. ✓ The trainings meant to be really good, it will be amazing! ✓ I thought I'd ask you because I know you like these kind of things and I mean can you imagine any of the others doing this? ✓ Aparently you get like a certificate after you've done it, it's a once in a lifetime oppertunity . ✓ I hope you can come, I'd really like to spend the day together, it will be a right laugh. ✓
Write back soon
Gemma

Some further information; spelling errors.

Informal conclusion; missing 'us'.

Examiner comment

The letter mixes formality and informality, though the informality is rather colloquial. The purpose of the letter is clear and there are some persuasive aspects to it; but the ideas are not well developed. There are few complex ideas. There are no paragraphs and the letter format is incomplete. There are some spelling and punctuation errors but it is mainly accurate. The writing fits Band 2 for content with a mark of five and Band 2 for accuracy with a mark of three.

The mark of 8/15 is borderline and indicates that the student would need further work on aspects of the writing to attain Level 2.

101

TestZone

Student C *Fail* X

No address or date offered; the name of the friend should be used.

Dear Friend ✓

For one of my birthday presents I got vouchers to do a parachute jump and I would like you to have my other voucher and come parachute jumping with me everything is already Paid for and the Training will be really good! ✓ it will defiantly help us with the jump, it will be great if you haven't done this evan if you have it will be really good I cant wait to do it. ✓ I have asked you becaus you are Fun and isn't scared of try new things. ✓ And your t scared of heights. ✓ You will be really proud of yourself because you will be daring yourself to do it everone of your friends will be jelous because you had the chance ✓

loads of love

Information given related to the topic in the task; the request is made; weak sentence structure; misuse of capitals; appropriate use of exclamation mark.

Capital 'I' in the first 'it' needed; 'definitely' misspelled; 'even' misspelled; there should be three sentences demarcated in this section or a well-constructed complex sentence.

Misplaced capital in 'Fun'; agreement error; 'try' is incorrect.

This sentence should be incorporated into the previous one for clarity and grammatical accuracy; common error with 'your'.

Sentence demarcation needed; spelling errors.

Examiner comment

The student has understood the task and presented information with some persuasion.

Although the letter is to a friend, it remains a functional communication and requires a letter format and salutation. The readership of the letter is only partly clear and the writing lacks development.

The content of the letter would be in Band 2 with a mark of four. The writing shows ability only in Band 1 of the accuracy part of the mark scheme with a mark of one.

A total mark of 5/15 would not achieve Level 2.

Peer/Self-assessment activity

1 Compare the answers you and your partner wrote with the student who gained a mark that would achieve Level 2 (Student A).
   ▶ Did you write your address fully on the right-hand side of the page?
   ▶ Did you use any interesting words, phrases and ideas to persuade your friend?

2 The task was to persuade. Find the parts of your letter, and your partner's letter, which you think are persuasive.
   ▶ Which words, ideas and phrases make them persuasive?
   ▶ Write down the ways you could improve the persuasive content.

3 Re-read the letter written by Student B. This student was close to getting a Level 2.
   ▶ How would you improve the way sentences 4 and 6 of Student B's letter are written?
   ▶ In what way is your letter clearer or more interesting than Student B's?

4 Find some examples of good sentences in your letter.
   ▶ What kind of sentences are the best ones?
   ▶ With your partner, find one example of a simple, compound and complex sentence in each other's work.
   ▶ Discuss with your partner what is wrong with the sentences used by Student C. How would you improve them?

Skill standard

Make a range of contributions to discussions in a range of contexts, including those that are unfamiliar, and make effective presentations.

What you need to do:

▶ Consider complex information and give a relevant, cogent response in appropriate language.

▶ Present information and ideas clearly and persuasively to others.

▶ Adapt contributions to suit audience, purpose and situation.

▶ Make significant contributions to discussions, taking a range of roles and helping to move discussion forward.

Your teacher or tutor will help you to decide whether to use the following task. They will also help you to organise the task should you attempt it.

Task: Discussion

Gang and knife or even gun culture among young people is rarely out of the news. There may be a number of reasons for the rise in this kind of activity:

▷ lack of parental control

▷ lack of respect for parents, peers or the authorities

▷ the influence of the Internet, videos or even some television

▷ peer group pressure

▷ drug-related issues

▷ influence from some aspects of American culture, e.g. rap music

▷ there being nothing else for people to do.

1   Your group needs to discuss the topic and possible reasons outlined above.
2   You might add to the list of issues.
3   Each person might take one of the issues listed above and find out what they can in preparation for a discussion on the topic.
4   The discussion will need an organising chairperson.
5   Remember:

   ▷ listen to others' ideas so as to make a relevant response

   ▷ to try to make a significant contribution to the discussion

   ▷ you could adopt a role in order to put ideas across.

6   The group should try to come to some conclusions about how things might be improved.

preparation and guidance

In this chapter you will find a Level 1 test of Reading and Writing and a Level 2 test of Reading and Writing.

Level 1 Reading

You will have 45 minutes to complete the Level 1 test. The test is in two sections. Section A contains six multiple choice questions on Source A. Each question has four possible answers but only one is correct.

Section B contains two questions on Source B, for which you will have to write the answers. You are allowed to use a dictionary.

The instructions will guide you through the test and provide you with spaces to write your answers.

Remember these things:

▶ Read the source texts through carefully, twice.

▶ Read all of the questions through for each section before you start to answer that section.

▶ Think carefully about each answer.

▶ For the multiple choice questions, don't try to guess, put in random answers or assume there is a sequence to the answers.

Level 1 Writing

You will have 45 minutes to complete the Level 1 Writing test. There are two questions. You must answer them both.

The instructions will guide you through the test and provide you with spaces to write your answers.

Remember these things:

▶ Read the task carefully.

▶ Note the scaffolding which is suggested.

▶ Write a plan before you write your answers.

Level 2 Reading

You will have 1 hour to complete the Level 2 test. The test is in two sections. Section A contains 12 multiple choice questions on Sources A and B. Each question has four possible answers but only one is correct.

Section B contains four questions on Sources A, B, and C, for which you will have to write the answers. You are allowed to use a dictionary.

The instructions will guide you through the test and provide you with spaces to write your answers.

Remember these things:

▶ Read the source texts through carefully, twice.

▶ Read all of the questions through for each section before you start to answer that section.

▶ Think carefully about each answer.

▶ For the multiple choice questions, don't try to guess, put in random answers or assume there is a sequence to the answers.

Level 2 Writing

You will have 1 hour to complete the Level 2 Writing test. There are two questions. You must answer them both.

The instructions will guide you through the test and provide you with spaces to write your answers.

Remember these things:

▶ Read the task carefully.

▶ Write a plan before you write your answers.

▶ Use good English and clear presentation.

▶ Check your work carefully.

Level 1 Reading test

For this Reading test you are going to read **two** texts. They are both about helping people.

Section A

Read Source A, called *Starlight*. This leaflet is being given to people in your area. You have been asked to find out how successful it is in getting across information by answering the questions that follow.

Source A

Starlight grants wishes of a lifetime to seriously ill children; and entertains children with fun and laughter in every hospital throughout the UK. Happy children respond better to treatment and each year Starlight helps over half a million children to forget about their illness and simply have a bit of fun. You can help make a Starlight wish come true by sending us money.

Olive's story

When Alex asked her six year old daughter Olive what her greatest wish would be, Olive said:

'I wish...to bake a cake for the Queen!'

Olive was diagnosed with leukaemia when she was just three years old. She has undergone years of treatment.

As soon as Starlight heard what Olive had wished for, plans were put in place to make sure that her wish came true in the most wonderful way. Before Olive knew it, she had received an invitation to Gordon Ramsay's house to bake a cake for Her Majesty the Queen! As soon as the cake was iced and decorated, Olive got ready to visit Buckingham Palace. At Buckingham Palace, Olive and her family were received by Starlight Patron, HRH Princess Alexandra, who was delighted to accept Olive's cake on behalf of Her Majesty the Queen.

Laughter is the best medicine

Every year Starlight brightens the life of over half a million sick children. Starlight does not receive funding from the government or the Lottery so depends on people like you. You can help children have a fun and enjoyable time:

 £12 gives a child in hospital a chance to escape to a Starlight party

 £25 pays for two children to laugh their way through a Starlight pantomime

 £250-500 means a very ill child can meet their favourite celebrity and get the full star treatment.

Whether you make a personal donation, hold an event or a sponsorship, every penny will make a big difference.

Please make Starlight your charity by visiting www.starlight.org.uk

Now answer the questions. Each of questions 1–6 is followed by four answers, A, B, C and D. For each question, select the right answer and mark its letter on your answer sheet.

1 The main point being made in the first section of blue writing is that Starlight:

   A buys hospital equipment for sick children
   B pays the doctors who treat children
   C helps children forget about their illness
   D raises half a million pounds every year.

2 In this section it also says that:

   A children that are happy respond better to treatment
   B half a million children are ill each year
   C there are children in every hospital throughout the UK
   D most hospitals provide entertainment.

3 The text tells you that Olive's wish was to:

   A meet Gordon Ramsay
   B bake a cake for the Queen
   C meet Princess Alexandra
   D visit Buckingham Palace.

4 The main point in the **'Laughter is the best medicine'** section is to:

   A inform you how much hospitals cost
   B tell you what the government pays for
   C show you what your money will buy
   D persuade you to donate at least £250.

5 In this section it tells you that:

   A Starlight gets money from the Lottery
   B meeting a celebrity costs most money
   C children like going to the pantomime
   D Starlight does not need any more money.

6 What the writer of the leaflet most wants you to do now is:

   A make Starlight your charity and raise money
   B visit the children in your local hospital
   C bake a cake and send it to the Queen
   D organise a school trip to Buckingham Palace.

Section B

Now read Source B, which is a webpage, and answer the questions that follow.

The questions in this section are testing what you have understood about the text. The questions are not testing your writing.

Source B

BritishRedCross

| In the UK | Overseas | About us | Get involved | Donate now | Shop |

Young volunteers help their neighbours

Young people in Wigan are signing up for a new project that helps ensure their elderly neighbours keep safe, warm and well.

The dawn patrol service – a pioneering Red Cross initiative that involves schoolchildren regularly looking out for their elderly neighbours – has been given £230,000 by the Big Lottery Fund.

Photograph courtesy of Layton Thompson/ British Red Cross

The service is simple to run yet very effective. Each morning, elderly people place a numbered indicator in their front windows, which young volunteers check on their way to school. If an indicator is missing or incorrect, the young person gets in touch with a designated adult who then checks out the situation.

Safe and secure

Each young patroller looks after three residents, handing over patrol duties to adult volunteers during school holidays and weekends. The project helps the older community continue living independently, secure in the knowledge that someone is regularly looking out for them.

The new Lottery-funded initiative will also offer home visits, and arrange for professional safety and fire checks to be made. Even better, a regular newsletter will provide vital information on fire hazards, avoiding bogus callers and how to keep warm in winter.

John Sutherland, operations director said: 'We're delighted that our dawn patrol service is getting this fantastic boost and we look forward to making a difference to the many elderly people in Wigan who will benefit from the investment in their welfare.

'This unique service also engages young people from local schools and teaches important aspects of social responsibility. And with five years' funding we'll be able to support vulnerable communities in Wigan for the foreseeable future.'

7 Use **all** of the information and ideas in the webpage to write a handout, to be given to students in your local schools to help them understand how their elderly neighbours could be looked after.

You should include:

- four things you've learned about how the Dawn Patrol works in Wigan
- four ways your elderly neighbours can be looked after.

You should write one sentence for each, using the spaces below.

- Four things about how Dawn Patrol works:

1 _____

_____

2 _____

_____

3 _____

_____

4 _____

_____

(4 marks)

- Four ways our elderly neighbours can be looked after:

1 _____

_____

2 _____

_____

3 _____

_____

4 _____

_____

(4 marks)

8 Look again at the **Starlight** leaflet. Look at the way it has been presented.

List **two** ways the Starlight leaflet has been presented and say **why each one** would make it easy for young people to understand.

1 First way presented:

_____

This makes it easy to understand because:

_____

(2 marks)

2 Second way presented:

_____

This makes it easy to understand because:

_____

(2 marks)

Level 1 Writing test

Question 1

This notice has appeared on your school or college notice board:

ADVENTURE Week

Your chance to enjoy a whole week of sailing, surfing, rock climbing, walking and much more in Devon.
You will be staying in a hostel with other students from the school.

- You can learn new sports.
- You will need to help with cooking and other chores.
- You will need to join in the evening's entertainment.

We are looking for students who can join in, get on with others and have something entertaining to offer.

If you are chosen ....it's FREE!

Write a letter to Mr Jones, the Head of Geography, applying to be accepted on the Adventure week.

Inform Mr Jones about:

- why you want to go on the adventure week
- what you have to offer.

Remember to:

- plan your answer
- write accurately in sentences and paragraphs.

Dear Mr Jones,

_____

_____

_____

_____

_____

_____

_____

_____

_____

_____

_____

(10 marks)

Question 2

Your cycling club is going to put out a leaflet about being safe on your bike.

This is the front page of the leaflet:

Your job is to finish the leaflet.

Write the text of the leaflet which will help people to cycle safely.

Write about:

- having a bike in good condition and wearing the proper gear
- how to ride safely on busy roads
- how to obey the rules of the road.

Remember to:

- plan your answer
- write accurately in sentences and paragraphs.

Write your leaflet:

_____

_____

_____

_____

_____

_____

_____

_____

_____

_____

_____

(10 marks)

Level 2 Reading test

For this exam you are going to read **three** texts. They are all about eating and health.

Section A

Read Sources A and B. You are taking part in a survey of young people in your area about eating and health. You have been asked to find out how effective the article and webpage are by answering the questions that follow. Each question 1 to 12 is followed by four answers A, B, C and D. For each question, select the right answer and mark it on the answer sheet provided.

Source A

Organic food

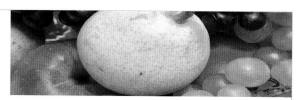

What does it mean?

Supermarkets and food shops offer organic food, often placed on separate shelves to ordinary or conventional foods. The most obvious organic foods are fruit, vegetables and meat.

What makes food organic?

The answer is the way it is grown or reared. Organic foods are produced in a way that limits the use of chemicals, pesticides and, in the case of animals, limits the use of growth hormones and antibiotics. People who believe in organic food say that your vegetables are grown in a clean, natural way and your meat comes from animals reared humanely and fed a healthy diet.

For hundreds of years all food was produced in a way that could be called organic because it wasn't till the 20th century that we discovered and used chemicals in farming.

What is good about it?

People who are enthusiastic about organic food say that it is good to eat because it's higher in nutrients — vitamins and minerals — and lower in bad things such as pesticide residues. They also claim that organic farming is good for the environment because farmers do not use chemicals which could harm other wildlife. Also, organic farming helps to increase plant and insect life while reducing waste.

Why should I eat it?

Here are some reasons:

- organic food is produced in a healthy way
- you are helping to keep the countryside natural and chemical-free
- it is more nutritious
- it tastes better.

What are the down sides?

Some critics of organic farming point out that much more space is needed to produce the same amount of food as conventional farming. If this is true, on a world-wide basis, organic farming would need to take over rainforests and other eco-systems to produce enough food. Because of the use of lots of space and labour, organic food is up to 40% more expensive than conventional products.

More information

If you are interested in organic food, there are lots of books, food articles in magazines and websites you could visit. The organisation responsible for setting the standards for organic food in the UK is Defra. Their website is full of information and news.

Questions 1–6 refer to Source A.

1 The main purpose of the article is to:

   A persuade you to eat organic food

   B inform you about organic food

   C describe dangers to the environment

   D explain why eating meat is bad for you.

2 The article says that:

   A lots of chemicals are used in organic food production

   B animals need antibiotics when they get ill

   C organic vegetables are grown in a clean, natural way

   D organic farming began in the 20th century.

3 The article tells you that people who are enthusiastic about organic food:

   A claim that it benefits the environment

   B believe there are too many nutrients in our food

   C encourage pesticide residues in farming

   D say that organic farming helps to control wildlife.

4 The article is suggesting that:

   A not enough chemicals are used in food production

   B supermarkets are making too much profit out of food

   C we need more laws in the UK to protect wildlife

   D there is some evidence that organic farming is best.

5 The article informs you that:

   A there are no reasons for you to eat organic food

   B conventional farming takes up more space than organic

   C organically produced food is more expensive than conventionally produced food

   D organic and conventional farming produce the same amount of food.

6 A suitable response to reading the article would be to:

   A persuade local farmers to go organic

   B find out more about organic food from Defra

   C send a donation to an animal charity

   D complain to your local supermarket about the price of food.

Source B

Home | Healthy diet | Age & stages | Health issues | Food safety | Food labels | Search

Eating for exams

When you're busy revising and thinking about your exams, it's easy to forget about eating healthily and to just reach for the nearest piece of food. But eating properly is just as important as revising properly – and can actually help you to revise better.

Like revision, eating healthily should start well before your exam but – also like revision – it's never too late to start.

Eat healthier snacks

Make sure you have healthier snacks with you while you're revising, to help keep you going. Snack foods such as cakes, biscuits, chocolate and sweets can be high in sugars and saturated fat, and low in certain vitamins and minerals. Instead, pick up an apple, some grapes, a currant bun or malt loaf with lower-fat spread. Always check the label and choose food that is lower in fat (especially saturated fat), sugars and salt.

Drink plenty of fluids

If you're feeling tired and lethargic while trying to revise, you might not be drinking enough water. Our bodies need water or other fluids to work properly. It's very important to make sure we're drinking enough. In climates such as the UK's, we should drink approximately 6 to 8 glasses (1.2 litres) of fluid every day to stop us getting dehydrated, so keep a glass of water on your desk and take a bottle of water into the exam if you can.

Drinks that contain caffeine, such as tea, coffee and cola, can act as mild diuretics, which means they make the body produce more urine. This affects some people more than others and also depends on how much caffeine you drink and how often. It's fine to drink these sorts of drinks, but you should also drink some fluids each day that don't contain caffeine.

Questions 7–12 refer to Source B.

7 The main purpose of this webpage is to:

   A inform you that eating fruit is good for you

   B advise you not to get stressed about exams

   C encourage you to make a full revision plan

   D persuade you to eat properly when revising.

8 The webpage states that:

   A it's easy to forget about exams when revising

   B eating properly can help your revision

   C it's more important to eat than to revise

   D sometimes it's too late to start your revision.

9 The webpage tells you that:

   A you shouldn't eat and revise at the same time

   B it's fine to snack on cakes, biscuits and cola

   C low fat food is the best food for revision time

   D it's normal to feel tired when you are revising.

10 The webpage informs you that:

   A if you feel tired while you're revising, you might be dehydrated

   B it's important not to drink too much water

   C you are not allowed water in an exam

   D revising makes you dehydrated.

11 The webpage suggests that:

   A it doesn't really matter what you eat or drink

   B you won't pass your exams unless you revise

   C caffeine drinks are not really very good for you

   D it's difficult to revise given the climate in the UK.

12 A good response to reading this webpage would be:

   A give up sweets, cakes and food that contains salt

   B think carefully about what you eat when revising

   C don't leave revising for your exams till it's too late

   D keep in touch with your friends at revision time.

Section B

Now read Source C and answer the questions that follow. Write your answers in the spaces provided. The questions are testing what you have understood about the text. They are not testing your writing.

Source C

Getting Active

Feeling a bit sluggish? Getting more active, alongside a healthy diet, is a great way to burn extra calories, help you lose weight and give you more energy. When we eat more food than our body uses during the day, it gets stored, usually as fat, and we put on weight. Here are some practical tips to help you get more active, choose a healthier diet and burn that excess energy.

Getting started

Getting going is half the challenge. So, if you're thinking about stepping up your activity levels, here are some simple ideas to get you started:

✳ Go for a walk – a brisk walk can make you feel good and it's free. Leave the car at home for those short journeys or get off the bus a stop early.

✳ Get out in the garden or go to the park. Take a football, a frisbee or a bat and ball. You don't need lots of fancy sports equipment to get out and have fun.

✳ Swimming is great exercise for all ages. Discounts and even free sessions might also be available at certain times for older people, children and families on income support.

It's a good idea to do something active every day, but you don't need to join a gym to do this if you don't want to. Try building up slowly and aim for at least 30 minutes of moderate intensity activity five times a week. Moderate intensity means that you feel warm and slightly out of breath, but are still able to hold a light conversation during the activity. But remember, any increase in your activity levels is an improvement and means you're already making a good start.

Whatever you choose to do, make sure you think about your safety. Check with your GP before you get started, they might also be able to give you some tips on what will work best for you.

Sticking with it

Fad exercises are usually hard to keep up, so try to pick an activity you enjoy and make it part of your daily or weekly routine, that way you're much more likely to stick with it. It's also a good idea to plan to do an activity with a friend or relative, having that extra support might just help you stick to your plan.

Refer to **Source C** to answer the following questions.

13 Sometimes texts have more than one purpose (e.g. *to explain, to inform, to describe, to argue, to advise*). Find two purposes which the *Getting Active* leaflet has and then select some text to support what you find.

First purpose _____

One example of this purpose is: _____

Second purpose _____

One example of this purpose is: _____

(4 marks)

14 You are going to write a handout for students at your school or college advising them about exercising to keep fit. Look again at the information given in Source C, the *Getting Active* leaflet, to help you.

Write 6 items in your handout.
- use **only** the material you have read from the leaflet
- select the information and advice you think people should know
- remember you are being tested on what you understand from reading the text, **not** on your writing skills.

Your handout:

1 _____

2 _____

3 _____

4 _____

5 _____

6 _____

(6 marks)

Questions 15 and 16 are about **Source A** and **Source B**.

15 You are taking part in a school or college project called 'The way people eat' to give young people information and ideas about eating habits.

Look again at Sources A and B. These sources offer information, advice and arguments about eating. Select ideas and information from Sources A and B that will help you with writing your project, recording them on the lines provided:

_____

_____

_____

_____

_____

_____

_____

_____

_____

(6 marks)

16 You now have to answer a question which compares two of the source texts you have read.

Look again at Source A and Source B. Explain which text you think has used presentational devices most effectively, providing two examples with reasons for your choices.

Overall I think the most effective text is Source _____.

First example of an effective presentational device with a reason why it is good:

_____

_____

Second example of an effective presentational device with a reason why it is good:

_____

_____

(4 marks)

Level 2 Writing test

Question 1

ABC Online Video Games
- Best value on the Net
- Hundreds of titles
- Money-back guarantee
- Back-up and advice
- Why pay more??

You ordered a video game from the company called *ABC Online Video Games* through their website. However, when it arrived it did not work properly and has damaged your machine.

Write an email to the company's customer services department, telling them about your experience and that you are dissatisfied.

You should try to persuade *ABC Online Video Games* to compensate you.

Remember to:

- plan your answer
- write in sentences and paragraphs
- check your spelling carefully.

Write on the form provided.

To:	customerservices@ABConlinevideogames.com
From:	
Subject:	

(15 marks)

Question 2

Here is the front page of a leaflet about what's going on in your school, outside of lessons.

The head teacher of your school or college has asked you to write the text for the above leaflet, which tells new students about the different activities they can do in school – apart from lessons – and which encourages them to join in.

Write the text for the leaflet for new students, informing them of the activities they can choose from and encouraging them to join in.

Remember to:

- plan your answer
- give some detail and be persuasive as well as informative
- write in sentences and paragraphs.

_____

_____

_____

_____

_____

_____

_____

_____

_____

_____

_____

_____

(15 marks)

Heinemann is an imprint of Pearson Education Limited, a company incorporated in England and Wales, having its registered office at Edinburgh Gate, Harlow, Essex, CM20 2JE. Registered company number: 872828

www.pearsonschoolsandfecolleges.co.uk

Heinemann is the registered trademark of Pearson Education Limited

Text © Pearson Education Limited 2010

First published 2010

12 11
10 9 8 7 6 5 4 3 2

British Library Cataloguing in Publication Data
A catalogue record for this book is available from the British Library on request.

ISBN 978 0 435151 40 9

Designed produced by Kamae Design, Oxford
Original illustrations © Pearson Education Limited 2010
Illustrated by Rory Walker
Cover design by Wooden Ark
Picture research by Virginia Stroud-Lewis
Cover photo/illustration © Peter Gridley. Getty Images
Printed in Malaysia, CTP-KHL

Acknowledgements
The author and publisher would like to thank the following individuals and organisations for permission to reproduce photographs

© iStockphoto/pmphoto pp2–3; © The Bridgeman Art Library p8; © Alamy/Justin Kase zsixz p18 (bottom);© Alamy/Bubbles Photolibrary/ John Powell (top left); © Corbis·p18 (top right); © Alamy/StockShot/ Dave Willis p19; © Blackburn with Darwen Borough Council pp20 (top), 21, 39; © Shutterstock/icyimage p20 (bottom); © Shutterstock/ Paul Reid p32 (left); © Getty Images/AFP pp33, 37; © Corbis/Matthew Ashton/AMA p35; © Rex/Dave Allocca p38 (right), 40; © Corbis/ Diego Azubel/epa p40 (bottom left); © Royal Mail p49 (top); © Classic Media 2009 pp49 (bottom), 51 (right), 52; © Getty Images/David Oliver pp54 (top), 114 (top); © Corbis/Bernd Vogel p54 (middle); © Alamy/Jeff Morgan Education p54; © Corbis/H. Benser pp60–61, 69; © Alamy/Peter Titmuss p62 (left), 72; © shutterstock/J. Helgason pp64, 65; © Alamy/Motoring Picture Library/National Motor Museum p66; © Alamy/Turkey pp70–71; © Shutterstock/michael Sheehan p78 (top left); © Alamy/Alex Segre pp78 (bottom left), 84; © Alamy/ Richard Levine p78 (top right); © Oxford University Press p80 (top); © iStockphotos/Rellas p81 (top); © Shutterstock/Adrian Hughes p81 (bottom); © Alamy/Nigel Lloyd p83; © Shutterstock/Kirill Kurashov p92; © iStockphotos/benjamin albiach p95 (top left); © David Davies/ PA Wire/Press Association Images p95 (bottom right); © Alex Segre / Alamy p97; © Monkey Business Images. Shutterstock p106; © Layton Thompson/British Red Cross p108; © Corbis/Radius Images p110; © Getty Images/Universal Images Group / Diverse Images p111; © D.aniel. Shutterstock pp112, 114 (middle); © Stanislav Fridkin. Shutterstock p114 (bottom); © Alamy/Max Bolotnikov p116; © Science Photo Library/Johnny Greig p118; © Corbis/Barry Lewis/In Pictures p119 (left); © Corbis/Peter Dench/In Pictures p119 (right).

Every effort has been made to contact copyright holders of material reproduced in this book. Any omissions will be rectified in subsequent printings if notice is given to the publishers.

Extracts from the Duke of Edinburgh website. Reproduced by permission of The Duke of Edinburgh's Award pv and p54; Chart from Deloitte Football Money League 'Top 20 Highest Revenue Generating Football Clubs in the World'. Reproduced with permission of the Deloitte Football Money League piv-v and p35; Extract from a leaflet entitled 'Could this be the shape of things to come?'. Reproduced with permission of Practical Action. P5, 6, 9 and 10; Blueprint diagram and text from a leaflet created by CAFOD. Reproduced with permission of CAFOD. P12; Careersforyou.com p20; Leaflet about homeless children in Bogo, article from Y Care International (YMCA). P22; Kids against Tobacco Smoke website. Roy Castle Charity. P26; Extract from efestivals website. Reproduced with permission of efestivals. P32 and p36; Cartoon: 'Have you any other references apart from your mother's?'. Source:www.CartoonStock.com. Reproduced with permission. P32; 'Fur companies lure designers' 21 March 2009, reproduced by permission of The Times. © The Times / nisyndication. com. P38; Extracts from the Vegetarian Society, from www.vegsoc. org. Reproduced by permission of the Vegetarian Society. P42; French egg-shaped buggy could spell the end of the humble British postman on his bike, article from The Daily Mail. Reproduced with permission. P49 and p52; Fire Safety Leaflet produced by MAST. Reproduced with permission of the Manitoba School Boards Association. P64; 'The Hobbit' by J.R.R. Tolkien, © 1993. Reproduced with permission of Harper Collins Publishers Ltd. P71; Cover from 'Concise Oxford English dictionary (11th ed., rev.)' by Soanes Catherine, Stevenson Angus (2009). Reproduced by permission of Oxford University Press. P80; Extract from National Rail's leaflet 'Disabled Persons Railcard, Rail travel made easy'. Reproduce with permission of National Rail. P83; Andrex advert 'Hello Softie'. Reproduced with permission of Kimberly-Clark Europe Ltd. P90; Anti-Smoking advert 'I'm not scared of clowns'. Reproduced with permission of the NHS and Getty Images. P90; Advert for Cadbury Buttons. Reproduced with permission of Cadbury. P91; Extract from Starlight Children's Foundation Leaflet. Reproduced with permission of the Starlight. Copyright © Starlight Children's Foundation, www.starlight.org.uk and ©clairedavies.com. P106; Website extract from 'Young volunteers help their neighbours' including the use of the red cross emblem, reproduced by kind permission of the British Red Cross. P108; 'Eating for exams' extracts from the Food Standards Agency website. P 114; 'Eat well, Be well' extracts from the Food Standards Agency website. P116;

Websites
The websites used in this book were correct and up-to-date at the time of publication. It is essential for tutors to preview each website before using it in class so as to ensure that the URL is still accurate, relevant and appropriate. We suggest that tutors bookmark useful websites and consider enabling students to access them through the school/college intranet.